How to Pray the Dominican Way

TEN POSTURES, PRAYERS & PRACTICES THAT LEAD US TO GOD

Angelo Stagnaro

Foreword by Fr. Giles Dimock, OP, STD

PARACLETE PRESS
BREWSTER, MASSACHUSETTS

How to Pray the Dominican Way: Ten Postures, Prayers, and Practices that Lead Us to God

2012 First Printing

ISBN: 978-1-61261-165-5

Nihil Obstat: Reverend John Cush, STL, Diocesan Censor

Imprimatur: Most Reverend Nicholas Di Marzio, PhD, DD, Bishop of Brooklyn
June 13, 2011

Library of Congress Cataloging-in-Publication Data
Stagnaro, Angelo, 1962-
  How to pray the Dominican way : ten postures, prayers, and practices that lead us to God / Angelo Stagnaro ; foreword by Giles Dimock.
     p. cm.
  Includes bibliographical references (p.   ).
  ISBN 978-1-61261-165-5 (trade pbk.)
  1. Dominicans—Spiritual life. 2. Prayer—Catholic Church. I. Title.
  BX3503.S73 2012
  248.3'2—dc23   2012019793

10 9 8 7 6 5 4 3 2 1

Published by Paraclete Press
Brewster, Massachusetts
www.paracletepress.com

Printed in the United States of America

If you are what you should be,
you will set the whole world on fire.

—St. Catherine of Siena,
Dominican Tertiary, Doctor of the Church

FIRST WAY

Humbling oneself
before the
altar of God

SECOND WAY

Lying
prostrate
upon the
ground

THIRD WAY

Concentrating
upon the suffering
of the world
and one's death

FOURTH WAY

Contemplating
upon the crucifix
and
genuflecting

FIFTH WAY

Standing
before God

SIXTH WAY

Standing in the
cruciform position,
contemplating
Christ's Passion
and death and
praying the Rosary

SEVENTH WAY

Praying with
hands
held high in
humble
supplication

EIGHTH WAY

Spiritual
reading

NINTH WAY

Meditation
as preparation
to
contemplation

These nine ways all lead to the tenth—
contemplation, the perfect prayer.

Contents

Foreword

Most people (Dominicans included), when they come across the medieval manuscript of *The Nine Ways of Prayer of St. Dominic*, with the miniature illuminated illustrations of the prayer postures that St. Dominic used, tend to be impressed and edified by these postures that our saint used, but they see no practical applications of these to their lives. The curious would find them quaint, but even serious seekers and believing Christians, though impressed by the use that our holy Father made of these common medieval postures, would tend to shy away from trying them in their own prayer life.

Angelo Stagnaro not only encourages the reader to try these prayer postures for a week at a time, but he also gives very useful tips on how to get the most out of them while praying. He also uses the structure of *The Nine Ways of Prayer* as a framework to discuss various modes and approaches to prayer as suggested by the disposition the posture brings about. He is able to intelligently "unpack" each approach in simple, down-to-earth terminology. And so we examine together the Rosary, the Stations of the Cross, meditation in the Jesuit manner, the ancient mode of holy reading, or lectio divina, and the monastic meditation that disposes one for contemplation, which is treated in some depth.

I learned much while reading this book and would recommend it both to the seeker and the beginner as well as to the seasoned veteran of the battle of prayer.

Fr. Giles Dimock, OP, STD

Dominican House of Studies

Washington, DC

Introduction

Contemplata aliis tradere

—Dominican motto, "To hand the fruits of contemplation on to others"

This book is the result of many years of teaching mystagogy—the study of sacramental mystical experience to adult converts in the period after their full entrance into the Roman Catholic Church. It's a way to deepen the understanding of catechetical teachings and explore their own feelings about and experiences of the sacred rituals. I'm continually impressed with the quality of converts to the Church. I've encountered incredibly inquisitive minds.

For a long time in my teaching I devoted myself to concentrating mostly on the catechism. But as I came to know my students better, I realized that their conversions were not merely on an intellectual level, even though this is an important and possibly the first vehicle by which one is drawn to God. I found when speaking to my catechumens that, despite the intense intellectual training they received, the weekly Eucharist and periodic sacrament of Reconciliation was, in many cases, insufficient; they wanted more to develop their spiritual lives. They wanted something to tide them over between Sundays and the occasional Holy Day of Obligation. The Church normally requires Rite of Christian Initiation of Adults (RCIA) catechists to reserve mystagogic instruction for the time between Easter and Pentecost, but, having witnessed the spiritual hunger of my catechumens, I created time throughout the year to explore different prayer forms as part of their instruction.

When I was looking for the best way to portray the myriad of Catholic prayer forms to my students, my spiritual director gave me a copy of St. Dominic's *Nine Ways to Pray* to read. The forms of prayer described in the book were common and easily learned, and I liked the text for its structure, sensitivity, and conciseness. I believe that it can still speak to modern Christians, whether Roman Catholic or not.

St. Dominic lived in exciting times and responded to that excitement in a laudable, Christlike manner. I love his philosophy and outlook of catechesis, evangelization, faith, and zeal for living a virtuous life. He's not as popular among lay Catholics as is St. Francis of Assisi, his exact contemporary, but he is just as important for the history of the Church. Christendom would be a very different place today had he not confronted the heretical Albigensians in the thirteenth century with his masterful knowledge of theology and his commitment to living a life of evangelical poverty.

Among the Dominicans' many Latin mottos, one is particularly apt in this situation: *Contemplata aliis tradere*. It means, "To hand the fruits of contemplation on to others." This was my aim in writing this book. I have not changed Dominic's original text in any way; I have only expanded upon it and tried to make it more accessible to modern Christians.

A major motivating theme among Dominicans is the drive to find truth no matter where it may be found. God cannot be confined and His Truth is available to all. Not all can understand it and not all accept it, but it is there nonetheless. I offer this book to every seeker of that Truth. May we find Him in prayer.

A Biography of St. Dominic de Guzmán

Inflamed by zeal for God and supernatural ardor,
by your limitless charity and the fervor of a vehement
spirit, you consecrated yourself wholly with the vow
of perpetual poverty to apostolic observance and to
evangelical preaching.

—Blessed Giordano of Saxony, writing of St. Dominic[2]

Using a quote from an ancient document, Pope Benedict XVI once said of St. Dominic, "He always spoke with God and about God. In the life of saints, love of the Lord and of neighbor, the seeking of God's glory and the salvation of souls always go together."[1]

Dominic was born in Caleruega, a small town between Osma and Aranda de Duero in Old Castile, Spain, in 1170. He is often referred to as being from Osma, as that is where he was stationed as an Augustinian priest.

His mother, Juana, named him after St. Dominic of Silos, the patron saint of expectant mothers. According to an early biography written by Giordano of Saxony, Dominic's mother dreamed that a dog leapt from her womb carrying a torch in its mouth with the intent of setting the earth on fire. This is still a common motif in Dominican churches and in the saint's hagiography. This legend was played up by later Dominicans because of the pun of their Latin name, *Dominicanus,* which can be deconstructed to be *Domini canes,* meaning "the hounds of the Lord."

Dominic was educated by his maternal uncle, a priest, and in the schools and university of Palencia. In 1191, Spain suffered under a widespread famine, which affected everyone but most especially the poor. Dominic sold his clothes, furniture, and even his books, a precious commodity at the time, in order to help the suffering. When his friends questioned him on his actions, he responded, "Would you have me study off these dead skins, when men are dying of hunger?"

In his travels, Dominic became aware of two great challenges confronting the Church in his time: first, the un-evangelized people of northern Europe, and, second, the Albigensian heresy in southern France. It was these two great experiences that made St. Dominic interested in missionary work.

In 1194, at the age of twenty-five, Dominic joined the Augustinian Canons Regular in Osma. In 1203, he was part of a diplomatic mission sent to Denmark in order to secure a bride for Crown Prince Ferdinand. When they crossed the Pyrenees into southern France, Dominic encountered the Albigensians (also known as the Cathars), a heretical, gnostic/Manichean sect with dualist beliefs. The Albigensians had both men and women clergy even though they were against the idea of a priesthood or even ordination. They claimed to be vowed to celibacy and poverty, but there is no proof that they kept these public promises. The Albigensian inner circle, who called themselves "Perfects," abstained from procreation but not from sex, and they supposedly took only a bare minimum of food and drink. Ordinary followers of the Albigensians were not required to ascribe to this level of commitment. Their followers, despite their outward dedication to these ideas, were actually encouraged to practice the opposite. The Albigensians' heretical clerics were charlatans who had kept their followers under their thrall by pretending they had incredible magic powers and by ridiculing the pompous lifestyles of some Catholic clerics.

The heretical Albigensians had a Manichean outlook on the world. They believed in a dualist concept of the cosmos, that is, two creative principles, one good and the other evil. The evil one was responsible for creating the physical universe, thus imbuing it with his evil. Thus, anything physical was to be avoided. They rejected marriage, procreation, the Church's sacraments, Christ's Incarnation, and most of Christian theology. In fact, the Albigensians viewed suicide, euthanasia, and abortion as logical outcomes of their worldview, and as actions that would be for the ultimate good, consistent with their rejection of the physical world.

Dominic immediately understood the need to combat this heresy. He was assigned by the Bishop of Osma to preach to the Albigensians of southern France, but he noticed he was not making a great deal of headway against them. The Albigensian clerics emphasized their own moral and spiritual "superiority" to their followers by comparing themselves to the Catholic priests who sometimes ate and dressed lavishly. In 1208, Dominic was frustrated by the successive failures of the richly dressed and well-heeled clerics who sought to win the Albigensian faithful back to the Church and warned them:

It is not by the display of power and pomp, cavalcades of retainers, and richly-houseled palfreys, or by gorgeous apparel, that the heretics win proselytes; it is by zealous preaching, by apostolic humility, by austerity, by seeming, it is true, but by seeming holiness. Zeal must be met by zeal, humility by humility, false sanctity by real sanctity, preaching falsehood by preaching truth.

So Dominic and three Cistercian companions began itinerant preaching according to the Gospel ideal.

He called the twelve disciples together and sent them out two by two. He gave them authority over the evil spirits and ordered them, "Don't take anything with you on the trip except a walking stick—no bread, no beggar's bag, no money in your pockets. Wear sandals, but don't carry an extra shirt." He also told them, "Wherever you are welcomed, stay in the same house until you leave that place. If you come to a town where people do not welcome you or will not listen to you, leave it and shake the dust off your feet. That will be a warning to them!" (Mk. 6:7–11)

Dominic embraced a life of poverty and dedicated himself to preaching the Gospel to both believers and nonbelievers. He traveled and preached in the region for ten years, being successful with the ordinary people but not with Albigensian clerical charlatans, who had too much to lose to admit they were frauds.

Dominic's first followers all abandoned him as the rigors of their minimalist lifestyle together with a demanding preaching schedule soon overwhelmed them. Ultimately, however, Dominic gathered a number of men who remained faithful to his ministerial vision of active witness to the Albigensians—an approachable ministerial style, a life of apostolic witness, preaching, intellectual rigor with a popular approach, and a love and respect for tradition.

It was from these humble beginnings that Dominic's idea of an Order of Preachers developed. In 1215, Dominic took up residence along with six followers in a house in Toulouse. The little group organized themselves as a monastic community based on penance and common prayer. Bishop Foulques gave them authority to preach throughout Toulouse. Dominic based his new community on the rule of St. Augustine, placing a great deal of emphasis on theological study, prayer, and community life for his friars in order to prepare them for a life of preaching. Since those first days, the Dominicans have trained some of the best theologians, mystics, philosophers, scientists, and theologians the Church has known, including St. Albert the Great (Albertus Magnus), St. Thomas Aquinas, St. Vincent Ferrer, and St. Catherine of Siena.

In the same year, 1215, (when the Fourth Lateran Council was convened), Dominic and Bishop Foulques went to Rome to secure the approval of Pope Innocent III for their growing order. It was there that Dominic met St. Francis of Assisi for the first time. In December 1216, Pope Honorius III gave permission for "The Order of Preachers" (*Ordo Praedicatorum,* or OP), popularly known as the Dominicans, to be formed. Dominic soon made his headquarters at Rome although he traveled extensively throughout Europe to maintain contact with his friars. In January 1218, Dominic made his way to Bologna and decided to relocate his ministry there, probably because of the presence of the city's excellent university.

Dominic always rigorously practiced self-denial, including eschewing meat, frequently fasting, observing prolonged periods of silence, and refusing to sleep in a bed. He always selected the worst accommodations and insisted upon wearing the simplest and cheapest of clothing. During his travels he gave spiritual instruction to his companions or led them in prayers. As soon as he passed the limits of towns and villages, he would remove his shoes and walk barefoot until he got close to the next town. Sharp stones and thorns would not deter him. Rain, snow, wind, and cold and other discomforts would never make him complain. Instead, he only praised God all the more intensely.

Dominic required his friars to have a solid theological foundation, which necessitated they attend the finest universities in Christendom. In addition, he taught that all Christians, not just priests, monks, and nuns, had access to a profound, interior joy found in contemplating the beauty of God's Truth. This gave birth to one of his community's mottos, later made popular by the Dominican St. Thomas Aquinas and mentioned earlier: *Contemplata aliis tradere*, "Give to others the fruit of your contemplation."

In addition, Dominic believed profoundly in the value of intercessory prayer for the success of apostolic work. He understood contemplation to be the ultimate, tranquil abiding in the presence of God that must be integrated seamlessly into the lives of all human beings. (See the Tenth Way, below.) It is from this prayerfulness that one's virtue, the ability to develop a proper Christian life, and dedication to one's ministry spring forth. Without prayer, there is no chance for success in this world. As Scripture teaches us:

> If the Lord does not build the house, the work of the builders is useless; if the Lord does not protect the city, it does no good for the sentries to stand guard. (Ps. 127:1)

Dominic died on August 6, 1221, at the age of fifty-one, at the convent of St. Nicholas at Bologna. He refused to rest in a bed and, instead, chose to lie upon some sacking stretched upon the ground. With his last breath, he exhorted his friars to have charity for each other and for all mankind, to guard their humility, to make their treasure out of poverty, and "to speak only of God or with God." The Dominican community kept its word to their founder, as is evidenced by another popular Dominican motto: *Laudare, benedicere, praedicare* ("To praise, to bless, to preach").

St. Dominic was canonized in 1234 by Pope Gregory IX. His feast day is celebrated on August 8. He is the patron saint of astronomers, because his early witnesses spoke of a radiance in his forehead, which was portrayed iconographically as a star. His patronage also extends to the falsely accused, Bologna, and the Dominican Republic (the nation is named for him).

St. Dominic's
Nine Ways of Prayer

He received every man in the great bosom of charity
and, because he loved everyone, everyone loved him.
He made a personal law for himself of being joyful with
happy persons and of weeping with those who wept.

—Blessed Giordano of Saxony, writing of St. Dominic[2]

*T*he *Nine Ways of Prayer* of St. Dominic was written anonymously sometime between 1260 and 1288 in Bologna, the city in which Dominic died. Sister Cecilia of the Monastery of St. Agnes at Bologna, who personally knew Dominic (he had received her vows), was the source of this biographical information.

The original text is actually very short and is more historical and hagiographic than a how-to-pray book. Throughout it, the reader comes to appreciate how the life of prayer absorbed Dominic and was his principal focus. It was this prayerfulness that energized him to accomplish all that he did in his life, including founding the Order of Preachers and converting a large percentage of the Albigensians back to the faith.

The original manuscripts of *The Nine Ways of Prayer* were illustrated with tiny drawings to illustrate the various postures that St. Dominic took while he prayed. The *Codex Rossianus*, a Spanish manuscript preserved in the Vatican Library, is just one example of this; it is painted in vivid colors and still in excellent condition.

Over the centuries, *The Nine Ways of Prayer* has often been printed as a supplement to Theodoric of Apoldia's Life of St. Dominic, although the two documents are clearly separate. The confusion was the result of Conrad of Trebensee, Provincial of Germany. He first encountered *The Nine Ways of Prayer* during a general chapter meeting of the community in 1288. He brought a copy of the treatise to Germany and gave it to Theodoric, who was starting to work on Dominic's hagiography.

St. Dominic used these nine forms of prayer during the Mass, the Liturgy of the Hours, and mostly during private prayer in chapel and when he traveled. He was often seen in ecstatic moments as he dedicated a great deal of time in prayer. Above all else, this treatise is about how the soul is moved by the body and how the body responds in turn. To be specific, ecstatic prayer is not merely an experience for the soul. Rather, it affects both the soul and the body because the two are intimately connected. After all, Christians believe in the resurrection of the body and its ultimate reunification with the soul.

How to Pray the Dominican Way utilizes additional Christian prayer forms that I have incorporated into Dominic's nine prayer systems. Even though this is not historically accurate, I chose to include them to show the rich diversity of Christian prayer forms and their applicability to modern life. For example, you will notice that this book offers ten ways, rather than St. Dominic's traditional nine; the tenth prayer form, offered here, is a natural extension—the intended culmination—of St. Dominic's ninth way. He was a known mystic and contemplative and thus was completely familiar with the prayer form. It is, however, an exceptionally difficult subject to describe, and so, in writing, Dominic left it to the spiritual warrior to explore on his or her own with the help of a spiritual director and, of course, the workings of the Holy Spirit.

Examine the prayer forms in this book each in its own turn. Although not everyone is made for every prayer form, it's important to give sufficient time to explore each one described here. I recommend practicing each prayer form for at least a week. Someone who is easily bored and races through the forms won't see the beauty and the spiritual value of these prayer forms; those people risk mistaking themselves as already being "spiritually accomplished." Whether there are other forms of Christian prayer is irrelevant. St. Dominic and many millions of believers have attained a life of sanctity through the original nine. Try them all in succession, being patient with them and with yourself—even if they don't initially "speak to you" or "inspire you." You will learn a great deal about yourself, about prayer, and about God by following these simple instructions.

Why Is Body Prayer Important?

It might be tempting to refer to St. Dominic's prayer forms as a type of "Christian yoga," but this is both inaccurate and misleading. Yoga is a Hindu philosophy, a spiritual, mental, and physical discipline that involves exercises and breathing techniques for attaining bodily and mental control and offers well-being to those who engage in it. In practicing the forms of yoga, one strives to suppress all activity of body, mind, and will so that the self may realize its distinction from the physical world and thus attain liberation and spiritual enlightenment. Some yogis claim to have attained almost magical powers, such as levitating above the ground or generating enough heat from their bodies to melt ice, but in the West most people regard yoga practice as primarily a way to keep physically fit and reduce stress.

Christian spirituality, as we know, helps you to be present to God or to share God's love with the world. True spirituality empties you of your self-love, liberating you from your selfishness—thus making room for God's love. Yoga, on the other hand, seems to be equal measures of Eastern philosophy and physical exercise. One might feel more nimble and flexible after a session of yoga but no closer to Christian sanctity than you would if you had run a marathon.

So St. Dominic's ways of praying that involve the body are quite different from any sort of "Christian yoga." The value of these prayer forms involves the physical but has a significantly differing focus from the values of yoga. To illustrate this, consider that Christians can point out thousands of examples of physically ill and disabled individuals who have nevertheless attained the highest degrees of sanctity, including these:

- St. Thomas Aquinas was morbidly obese and suffered greatly from the effects of this eating disorder throughout his life. Despite this, he was an accomplished mystic and wrote the *Summa Theologica*, the singularly most important theological treatise in Christian history.

- St. Ignatius Loyola had a painful limp throughout his adult life after having been hit in the leg with a cannonball. Despite this, he was a mystic and managed to create a spirituality that has sustained the Jesuit order and those who have profited from their academic instruction and spiritual guidance. He wrote *The Spiritual Exercises,* which is the keystone of Ignatian spirituality.

✣ St. Thérèse of Lisieux died of tuberculosis at the age of twenty-four, but her prayer life sustained her throughout her suffering. Her spiritual autobiography, *The Story of a Soul*, has been an inspiration to millions.

✣ St. Bernadette Soubirous suffered from poor health since birth. Her asthma did not allow her to accomplish a great deal. Despite chronic health problems, including a very painful tumor on her leg, her prayer life, which included mystical revelations, sustained her throughout her suffering. St. Bernadette died at the age of thirty-five.

✣ Despite St. Teresa of Ávila's being afflicted with bodily ills throughout her life, her book *The Interior Castle*, her spiritual magnum opus, led countless people to pursue holiness by dedicating themselves to Christ, including people who weren't even Christian. St. Teresa Benedicta of the Cross (Edith Stein), Blessed Mother Teresa of Calcutta, and St. Thérèse of Lisieux all attributed their desire to serve Christ to reading Teresa's book. They all even took her name when they became nuns.

☙ Blessed Herman the Cripple was born with a cleft palate, spina bifida, and cerebral palsy to a poor German farming family and suffered greatly throughout his life because of his disabilities. At the age of twenty, he became a Benedictine monk. In addition to being a polymath and a polyglot, he is also the author of "Salve Regina" and "Alma Redemptoris Mater," two of Christianity's most beautiful poems.

☙ St. Lidwina of Schiedam remained bedridden from the age of fifteen as a result of having broken a rib while ice-skating. This was followed by a progressive illness (identified possibly as multiple sclerosis), and she was in inconceivable pain for the remainder of her life. She was said to have been near death twenty-two times before finally succumbing to her illness. Despite this, she was known as a living saint during her lifetime.

Of course, there are many others as well. None of these people enjoyed physical health. Clearly, praying with the body involves more than, or something other than, yogic flexibility.

In addition, most Christian martyrs, like the Savior Himself, died horrible painful deaths. St. Edith Stein and St. Maximilian Mary Kolbe were both tortured to death in Auschwitz. Christians between the first and third centuries often were publicly tortured, including being fed to lions and other wild beasts. St. Lawrence and St. Joan of Arc were burned alive. St. Catherine of Alexandria was beaten to death. St. Francis of Assisi experienced an intensely painful stigmata mirroring Christ's Passion upon the Cross. St. Isaac Jogues was tortured, mutilated, and beheaded by the Mohawks. Yoga's superficially expressed purpose, through bodily movement, is to make you "feel" good. That is not necessarily a Christian value.

Authentic Christian spirituality may or may not make you feel good, but it is designed to make you a good person. All people who have attained sanctity have one thing in common: specifically, they have emptied themselves of their self-destructive egos and dedicated themselves fully to God. The sure sign of success in this endeavor is the personal joy one experiences in prayer and the growth in virtue as one dedicates oneself to helping those in need. As Pierre Teilhard de Chardin reminds us, "Joy is the infallible sign of God's presence."

Physical health has never been considered a sign of holiness. If it were, we would logically need to conclude that physical disease and disability are signs of God's "disfavor." Throughout the New Testament, Jesus would heal people by forgiving them of their sins. It's odd in these self-indulgent and self-centered times that individuals obsessed about their bodily suppleness and physical flexibility would call themselves spiritual. It should also be pointed out that humanity is so flawed that we could never—even if we had thousands of lifetimes—attain any level of true sanctity by our own merits. This is the Christian view of the world and of true salvation. If we could develop our own sanctity, we wouldn't need God. If we could develop our own sanctity, the world would be a great deal nicer. And yet, this is clearly not the case. Perhaps yoga is, for most people, exercise and nothing more; but sometimes it may serve as a means by which people can actively avoid exploring an authentic, Christian spirituality.

Although St. Dominic's nine ways of prayer involve physical movements and postures, they are meant to unite body, mind, and soul, not to separate them. In a way, one could say that Dominic's prayer forms legitimize and sanctify bodily prayer by dedicating it to Christ. They aim to unite body, soul, and mind for the sake of becoming united with God, shedding your ego, and becoming a better person. Dominic's ways of prayer are, simply put, a simple but profound path to God.

The Need for Prayer in Our Lives

What's the use of calling ourselves Christians if we intentionally avoid speaking to, listening to, and relying upon Christ? Not to pray is to defeat the purpose of the sacraments, especially baptism.

If we lead our lives without even so much as a nod to our Creator and Redeemer, without acknowledging the precious gift of existence He generously gave us, why would anyone think spending an eternity with Him in heaven was something enjoyable or even preferable? In other words, if ten minutes in prayer a day is seen as an interminable and insufferable waste of time, what would you do with a timeless eternity before the Lord of All, not having already made His acquaintance while still alive?

More people would seek out prayer if they only knew of the inconceivable pleasures and consolations God bestows upon us when we seek Him through prayer. And with more people seeking His guidance and love in the embrace of divine ecstasy, there would be less interest in and opportunity for sin. Imagine an entire planet that was so properly engaged— the entire human race at one with its Maker. "Love and faithfulness will meet; righteousness and peace will embrace. Human loyalty will reach up from the earth, and God's righteousness will look down from heaven" (Ps. 85:10–11).

It can be said that the first step toward a life of prayer is not faith in God but, rather, the more important step of abandoning our love of self. Narcissism blinds and poisons us into thinking that we are self-sufficient—that we have no need for other beings or even the Being who gave us existence. A self-consumed person acts self-referentially and, worse, self-reverentially. A person who thinks so highly of himself refuses to recognize the vast, terrifying, festering emptiness that lies in wait for him in the center of his being. But in those dark, lonely moments, when we are at our most lucid, we come to the realization that we can't rely upon anything in this ever-changing world. Even those who rely upon the power, wealth, and prestige they've accumulated ultimately realize that life, in and of itself, is meaningless (Ps. 20:7). It is but an empty pursuit that leads to decay and then a lonely, terrifying death: "Life is useless, all useless" (Eccles. 1:2).

The rational person, realizing his weakness, intimately and intuitively understands that only through love can he come to true meaning and ultimate lasting happiness—that the infinite emptiness inside us can only be filled with Something that is infinite. And then it all begins to make sense. If God exists and is the Source of our being and love, our own spiritual emptiness makes sense. He created us as empty vessels into which He will gladly flow, filling us to capacity and then to overflowing. That love can wash over us, healing us, and then spill onto all those around us, filling and healing them as well. Only the Infinite can suffice to fill the empty space inside us.

How to Use This Book

Each of these forms of prayer is meant to be practiced for one week before moving on to the next one. Try and stick to this regimen if at all possible.

Also, to get the most out of this book, as well as Dominic's prayer forms, it is best to not skip any of the ten forms, but rather to explore each in turn and in its proper order.

These prayer forms brought St. Dominic to tears and inspired in him a love of Christ and His Blessed Mother. In other words, the prayer forms worked for him in the order and sequence in which he performed each of them. He didn't pick and choose which ones were "more fun" or appealing and neither should we. Many other great Christian mystics have learned from these prayer forms. Allow them to teach you fully.

Each of these ways of prayer connects body and soul. Your body reflects the changes in your soul and vice versa. This process requires both humility and patience. If you find a particular prayer form difficult, I recommend praying for humility and patience. Rushing through these ways of prayer is worse than worthless—it can be spiritually dangerous.

The only things you will need, beyond the book in your hands, are:

- Comfortable clothing
- A quiet place in which to pray
- A rosary (if you do not have a rosary, you may use the printed one on page 82)
- A Bible

Although it is true that Dominic prayed these nine forms of prayer before the altar, you aren't required to do so. St. Dominic could because he was St. Dominic and because he founded the Order of Preachers whose houses always had chapels. Most of us aren't that fortunate. Admittedly, you could ask permission of your pastor to pray in your parish's chapel, and that sometimes works well. However, the intensity of the prayer forms described in this book indicates they are best practiced in a private, secluded area, which can also be simply prepared in one's home. A prayer corner is easy to create and does not require the use of a construction crew. You can easily do it yourself. All you need is a crucifix or an icon in the corner of a room and a comfortable place to rest before it.

Keep in mind that this is sure to be an intense period of prayer for you. It's important to request the sacraments during the time you explore Dominic's forms of prayer. Ideally, you would attend daily Mass and receive the sacrament of Reconciliation once a week prior to receiving the Eucharist. This is not a requirement to explore these ways of prayer, but it is an important aid in developing any spiritual life. In addition, a spiritual director could help you understand the complexities that come up while you are deepening and developing your prayer life in these new ways. A confessor can also serve as a spiritual director if approached properly.

Set aside time every day for a week to concentrate on each prayer form. Very few people in modern society have the luxury of not having to do anything all day for ten straight weeks. Most of us have jobs and have children and spouses to care for. The prayer forms in this book are flexible enough to fit into even a very hectic schedule. If you only reserve thirty minutes immediately before going to bed, it would be sufficient at this point in your spiritual development. You may take longer than a week to explore each of the prayer forms, but do not take fewer than seven days. It takes some time to become comfortable with each prayer form. Not everyone is suited to every type of prayer, but it is important to allow the Holy Spirit to guide you as to how things are going to unfold in your life. St. Dominic, among countless other believers, grew in sanctity through these prayer forms. Allow the Holy Spirit to act through you in approaching these bodily experiences of prayer. If a particular one doesn't come easily to you, ask yourself—and the Holy Spirit—"Why?" Then take the time to listen. I've met many people who claim to be turned off to Christian prayer, but very few of them have actually put it into serious practice.

When praying, remember that you are not the active agent. You are emptying yourself so that God might pray inside your soul, or, more accurately, you are emptying yourself so that you might listen to God in the depths of your soul. This is not a sprint, but rather a long-distance race.

At the end of each prayer form is a scriptural passage. I recommend sitting down still in the presence of the Lord, before either the tabernacle, His altar, an icon, or a crucifix, and reading the passage silently. Meditate on it. Allow it to fill and heal your soul.

When you've finished exploring each prayer form, consider journaling about your experiences. Keeping a written record of your experiences during prayer will prove to be invaluable as you develop an authentic spirituality. Each chapter offers a small place to jot preliminary notes, but you should consider using a dedicated notebook or keeping an electronic file on your computer to record your observations. Journal about your successes, the impediments to prayer you've experienced, your visualizations, your insights, and anything else you would like, including thoughts you want to express to God.

How to Pray the Dominican Way

THE FIRST WAY OF PRAYER

Humbling Oneself
Before the Altar of God

This altar is a witness to all of us that the Lord is God.

—Joshua 22:34

❖ STRUCTURE OF PRAYER

The first way of prayer that Dominic used was the simplest. He would frequently use this to prepare himself for other, more complicated forms. The first way was to approach Christ, as symbolized by His altar, in a humble manner. He would approach the altar believing Christ was truly and personally present and not just a symbol: the Church understands the Eucharist to be His Real Presence.[3]

The path to God is through humility. Nothing else is acceptable. One must eschew power for oneself. Those preachers, teachers, or gurus who claim to have special spiritual "powers" insist that they also have the ability to wield them. A legitimate religion and true spirituality, on the other hand, requires that a person give up power, in order to become powerless—to submit to a Higher Power. If anyone believes themselves to have great mystical or magical powers, they don't need anything else, even God. St. Dominic fought against this sort of heresy espoused by the Albigensians during his lifetime, and so should we. "Spiritual" leaders hungry for power and money ultimately will offer you nothing of value and may rob you not just of your cash but also of your self-respect. True Christian spirituality is accomplished with less, not more. The further beauty of legitimate spirituality is that it is not complex. In fact, one has to discover one's true humanity, not a fountainhead of "hidden mystical power."

▓ HOW TO PRACTICE

- Stand before the altar of God and, with head bowed, humbly consider Christ.

- Lose yourself in the image of Christ exalted. Dominic taught his friars to do this whenever they saw an image of the Crucified One.

- Compare the state and quality of your soul with that of Christ.

Dominic would approach the altar using the following scriptural passages:

> Your power does not depend on the size and strength of an army.
> You are a God who cares for the humble and helps the oppressed.

You give support and protection to people who are weak and helpless; you save those who have lost hope.

(Jdt. 9:11)

"Lord, I am not worthy to have you come under my roof; but only speak the word, and my servant will be healed."

(Mt. 8:8 NRSV)

He leads the humble in the right way and teaches them his will.

(Ps. 25:9)

Humble yourselves before the Lord, and he will lift you up.

(Jas 4:10)

■ Be mindful of the Triune God Who created, redeems, and sustains you. Bow your head in respect and love and pray the Glory Be prayer slowly and reverentially.

Glory be to the Father, and to the Son, and to the Holy Spirit: As it was in the beginning, is now, and ever shall be, world without end. Amen.

■ Accept the humility God asks of you. Understand it as the sole means by which you may approach Him. Pride destroys all relationships, first and foremost the one between the soul and its Creator. Consider how you can try to remain humble in your everyday life.

✖ SCRIPTURE READING

O Lord, you are faithful to those who are faithful to you; completely good to those who are perfect. You are pure to those who are pure, but hostile to those who are wicked. You save those who are humble, but you humble those who are proud. O Lord, you give me light; you dispel my darkness. You give me strength to attack my enemies and power to overcome their defenses. This God—how perfect are his deeds! How dependable his words! He is like a shield for all who seek his protection. The Lord alone is God; God alone is our defense. He is the God who makes me strong, who makes my pathway safe. He makes me sure-footed as a deer; he keeps me safe on the mountains. He trains me for battle, so that I can use the strongest bow. O Lord, you protect me and save me; your care has made me great, and your power has kept me safe. You have kept me from being captured, and I have never fallen. (Ps. 18:25–36)

Lying Prostrate upon the Ground

> "God, be merciful to me, a sinner!"
>
> —LUKE 18:13, NRSV

✖ STRUCTURE OF PRAYER

St. Dominic would lie upon the floor before the altar and feel great remorse in his heart for his sins and the sins of the world, praying either aloud or silently as the Spirit moved him.

✖ HOW TO PRACTICE

You don't need to lie upon the floor of an actual church—this would probably attract too much unwanted attention. However, this is an excellent prayer to do in the privacy of your own home, in the forest, or on the beach.

Lying facedown upon the floor is a practical, humbling experience. The floor represents baseness, filth, and lowliness. It's not so bizarre to consider why St. Dominic chose the floor to humble himself.

■ Keep the image of the Magi encountering the Holy Family in mind.

They threw themselves to the ground and worshiped the Lord of All as he was held by His Immaculate Mother and His loving father, St. Joseph. The three great kings threw themselves to the ground before God and worshiped Him, saying: "Come, let us adore and fall down in prostration before God, and let us weep before God, and let us weep before the Lord that made us" (Ps. 94:61, from the original *Nine Ways to Pray*).

■ With these words (the first quote, below) of St. Dominic in mind, then pray the following scriptural passages slowly and reverentially:

I am not worthy to see the heights of heaven because of the greatness of my iniquity, for I have aroused Thy anger and done what is evil in Thy sight.
—St. Dominic

We fall crushed to the ground; we lie defeated in the dust. Come to our aid! Because of your constant love save us!
(Ps. 44:25–26)

I lie defeated in the dust; revive me, as you have promised.
I confessed all I have done, and you answered me; teach me
your ways.
(Ps. 119:25–26)

■ Be mindful of your sins, especially those sins that have inspired
sins in others around you.

■ Be sure to pray for others, especially those sinners who do
not recognize their sins. Pray the following scriptural passage
reverentially, either aloud or in the silence of your heart:

We have sinned, we have been evil, we have done wrong. We have
rejected what you commanded us to do and have turned away
from what you showed us was right.
(Dan. 9:5)

■ Now, pray the Jesus Prayer:

(Breathe in)   "Jesus Christ, Son of God . . ."
(Breathe out)   ". . . have mercy on me, a sinner."

The Jesus Prayer is a dynamic, life-affirming, simple, and succinct prayer. With a single intake of breath and its release, a Christian relates and affirms his or her belief in Jesus Christ as the Messiah, the Son of God, and the merciful, sacrificing Savior of sinful humans. The Christian who prays this prayer places himself in the proper, humble, and loving relationship with his Creator. The Jesus Prayer, also known as the Prayer of the Heart, is short and formulaic. Despite this, it is not a mantra, even though it is repeated continually.[4] It is similar to a Zen koan in that it invites the individual Christian to internalize prayer so that he becomes the prayer. In this way, the individual Christian may pray perpetually. Another similarity is that koans are not meant to be understood with the rational mind but rather with the soul.

This prayer form is accepted by many Christians, particularly Catholics, and is most highly revered and popular among Orthodox Christians. St. Gregory Palamas (1296–1359), Archbishop of Thessalonica and a monk trained at Mount Athos, wrote extensively on the Jesus Prayer and was a chief exponent of it, although it is certainly a great deal older than that. The prayer probably originated among the fifth-century Desert Fathers of Egypt.[5] The earliest known specific mention of the Jesus Prayer is in the writing of St. Diadochos of Photiki (400–c. 486), *On Spiritual Knowledge and Discrimination.* St. John Climacus (c. 523–606) also recommends using the prayer in his *Ladder of Divine Ascent.*

The Jesus Prayer is effectively the Orthodox Christian counterpart of the Roman Catholic Rosary. In fact, Orthodox Christians also use a type of prayer beads with the Jesus Prayer. This beautiful prayer is based on Christ's parable of the Publican and the Pharisee:

Jesus also told this parable to people who were sure of their own goodness and despised everybody else. "Once there were two men who went up to the Temple to pray: one was a Pharisee, the other a tax collector. The Pharisee stood apart by himself and prayed, 'I thank you, God, that I am not greedy, dishonest, or an adulterer, like everybody else. I thank you that I am not like that tax collector over there. I fast two days a week, and I give you one tenth of all my income.' But the tax collector stood at a distance and would not even raise his face to heaven, but beat on his breast and said, 'God, have pity on me, a sinner!' I tell you," said Jesus, "the tax collector, and not the Pharisee, was in the right with God when he went home. For those who make themselves great will be humbled, and those who humble themselves will be made great."

(Lk. 18:9–14)

The Pharisee, thinking himself spiritually perfect, doesn't thank God for His mercy and kindness but simply for making him perfect. The Publican, a Jew who collaborated with the authorities of the Roman Empire, especially in regards to extorting taxes from his fellow Jews, prays humbly and asks for forgiveness for his imperfections. The parable perfectly describes the correct attitude and relationship between the individual believer and his Creator.

To pray the Jesus Prayer, draw in a deep gentle breath while concentrating on the phrase, "Jesus Christ, Son of God." When ready to exhale, concentrate on the remainder of the phrase, "have mercy on me, a sinner." You will find after many days and weeks of using this prayer that you will unintentionally fall into the habit of saying it either silently (that is, mentally) or aloud. It will become as natural to you as your breathing or heartbeat. The experience is perfectly overwhelming.

As you practice it, consider the simplicity of the Jesus Prayer. Let the words seep into your heart and soul. Allow it to fill your being.

�֎ SCRIPTURE READING

Then once again I lay face downward in the Lord's presence for forty days and nights and did not eat or drink anything. I did this because you had sinned against the Lord and had made him angry. I was afraid of the Lord's fierce anger, because he was furious enough to destroy you; but once again the Lord listened to me. The Lord was also angry enough with Aaron to kill him, so I prayed for Aaron at the same time. I took that sinful thing that you had made—that metal bull-calf—and threw it into the fire. Then I broke it in pieces, ground it to dust, and threw the dust into the stream that flowed down the mountain. You also made the Lord your God angry when you were at Taberah, Massah, and Kibroth Hattaavah. And when he sent you from Kadesh Barnea with orders to go and take possession of the land that he was giving you, you rebelled against him; you did not trust him or obey him. Ever since I have known you, you have rebelled against the Lord. So I lay face downward in the Lord's presence those forty days and nights, because I knew that he was determined to destroy you. And I prayed, "Sovereign Lord, don't destroy your own people, the people you rescued and brought out of Egypt by your great strength and power. Remember your servants, Abraham, Isaac, and Jacob, and do not pay any attention to the stubbornness, wickedness, and sin of this people. Otherwise, the Egyptians will say that you were unable to take your people into the land that you had promised them. They will say that you took your people out into the desert to kill them, because you hated them. After all, these are the people whom you chose to be your own and whom you brought out of Egypt by your great power and might." (Deut. 9:18–29)

Concentrating upon the Suffering of the World and One's Death

Whenever anything disagreeable or displeasing happens to you, remember Christ crucified and be silent.

—St. John of the Cross

✛ STRUCTURE OF PRAYER

After using the second way of prayer, Dominic would rise from lying on the ground and would discipline himself, beating his body with an iron chain, and praying, "O Lord, you protect me and save me; your care has made me great, and your power has kept me safe" (Ps. 18:35). This sort of personal corporal discipline was common practice in thirteenth-century Spain. The penitential practices, joyfully accepted, were meant to bring us closer to God and strengthen our wills to serve Him. When we read about the early saints and martyrs, it cannot but seem that they were made of sterner stuff than we moderns (and chains are not part of the recommended practices of this book). Still, Don Bosco once warned Dominic Savio, the first Salesian saint, to not practice too many mortifications since life for a schoolboy was difficult enough as it was!

Francis Poulenc's *Dialogues des Carmélites* (1957) is an opera without a great deal of action, but it still has a very profound and riveting storyline. The curtain rises on a French Carmelite convent on the eve of the French Revolution, where the nuns are attending their dying abbess, who is suffering horribly in her final moments. The youngest nuns look upon her and wonder why it is that someone as holy as she should suffer so while truly evil people appear to suffer not at all. The theme of the opera is that we suffer not only for our sake but for the sake of others. If not, we would all become monsters unconcerned and uncaring of others. Pain and suffering save us from our darkest selves. The atheist who insists that the existence of pain and suffering in the world proves that God doesn't exist is most likely not the person who ever will pick up a ladle in a soup kitchen or donate money to help starving children.[6]

People who allow the pain and suffering in this world to enter their hearts and allow their hearts to become a crucible in which pain is transmuted into love are capable of extraordinary charity, kindness, and generosity. As Aeschylus writes:

And even in our sleep pain that cannot forget falls drop by drop upon the heart, and in our own despair, against our will, comes wisdom to us by the awful grace of God.

(*Agamemnon* 179–183)

That wisdom and its accompanying compassion, which comes to us by that terrible grace, stokes the engine of compassion, the human soul. Self-indulgence doesn't make us holy; consciously accepting the pain and suffering that comes into our lives does.

What does compassion and self-sacrifice mean? The greatest error and conceit of Western society is the illusion that you and I are separated and distinct. That we are, in fact, competitors. Pope John XXIII reminds us that "God created men as brothers, not foes." The moment we accept and understand this, it becomes easier to see God in others and to love them.

Although it may seem uncommon in our modern world, the truth is that many people eschew immediate gratification, including athletes, explorers, and humanitarians such as Mother Teresa. Words like "discipline" seem odd, old-fashioned, or simply weird in these modern days. But the truth is that many people have become saints because the Divine love they felt inspired them to practice physical mortification, fasting, avoiding complaining, almsgiving, and bearing slights and inconveniences with a smile. There are many saints to whom we can turn who have exemplified these behaviors, including Pope John Paul II, Mother Teresa, Dorothy Day, Peter Maurin, Terence Cardinal Cooke, St. Francis of Assisi, St. Josemaría Escrivá, and countless other saintly persons, but there are many ordinary Christians, too.

So in this chapter we will explore many spiritually enriching alternatives available to us through the third way of prayer.

Momento Mori

"Heaven and earth will pass away, but my words will never pass away. No one knows, however, when that day or hour will come— neither the angels in heaven, nor the Son; only the Father knows. Be on watch, be alert, for you do not know when the time will come. It will be like a man who goes away from home on a trip and leaves his servants in charge, after giving to each one his own work to do and after telling the doorkeeper to keep watch. Watch, then, because you do not know when the master of the house is coming—it might be in the evening or at midnight or before dawn or at sunrise. If he comes suddenly, he must not find you asleep. What I say to you, then, I say to all: Watch!"

(Mk. 13:31–37)

Memento mori is a Latin phrase that means "Remember your death." In ancient Rome, triumphant Roman generals would ask a slave to whisper in their ear the phrase "Memento mori" as the general received the adulations of the crowds. The practice kept the general humbled and grounded.[7] The phrase is meant to remind Christians of their own mortality with a strong emphasis on death, Divine Judgment, heaven, hell, and the salvation of the soul. To the Christian, the prospect of death serves to emphasize the vapid and ephemeral nature of earthly pleasures, luxuries, titles, and achievements. By so keeping one's mortality and the uncertainty of the time of one's death in mind, it thus becomes an invitation to focus on the afterlife. As Scripture teaches us:

> Whatever you do, remember that some day you must die. As long as you keep this in mind, you will never sin.
> (Sir. 7:36)

By remembering our eventual death, Christians understand this world will pass away. When an individual dies, as far as he's concerned the world has, in fact, ended. Spiritually speaking, an ounce of prevention is worth a pound of cure. The Church teaches that we should prepare ourselves to receive the sacrament of Anointing of the Sick at the end of our lives by receiving the sacraments of Reconciliation and the Eucharist often, by engaging in the acts of mercy, by living a virtuous life, by developing one's prayer life, and by resigning ourselves to God's will. By doing this, we will come to a happy end. After all, a wise and rational person anticipates the inevitable. It is not a sign of wisdom, let alone sanity, to continually put off the one thing that ultimately defines us as mortals. As Scriptures teach us:

> If you do no wrong, no wrong will ever come to you. Do not plow the ground to plant seeds of injustice; you may reap a bigger harvest than you expect.
>
> (Sir. 7:1–3)

✖ HOW TO PRACTICE

- With permission from your physician and your spiritual director, you should fast during the day you've set aside for prayer.

In the traditional Church rule for a fast day, this would mean one normal-size meal and two smaller "collations," that is, two smaller meals that wouldn't add up to an entire full meal. You are, of course, allowed all the fluids you need and any necessary medications. Your spiritual director can best help you plan this or any additional fasting you might like to add.

Fr. Jim Van Vurst, OFM, offered fascinating alternatives to the Lenten traditional fasting from food in a recent article titled "Jesus on Fasting and Penance." He suggests that we could give up (1) insisting we are always right in any argument; (2) controlling family members and others by means of anger or deadly silence; (3) relying on a clever but sarcastic tongue that we might think is cute but cruelly hurts others, even loved ones; (4) wasting hours on the Internet when we could be doing something with our family.

There are other examples, of course, but you may find that the above suggestions are much more challenging than simply cutting down on or eliminating some type of food.[8]

- Consider your death. In death we find life, and, in life, death will inevitably come.

Contemplating death involves intense and thorough, even painful, honest self-examination. The assistance of a trained and experienced spiritual advisor is very useful in keeping us from deluding ourselves both with being overly impressed with ourselves and with being overly scrupulous. A spiritual advisor will help us come to a better understanding of our faults and our strengths in a Christian context. Through self-examination and frequent reception of the sacrament of Reconciliation, we become purified of our sins and our sinfulness. In order to bring our mortality into your meditation, consider using the following exercise.

Imagine yourself on your deathbed.

Who would you hope is attending you?

What are they saying to you?

Are you afraid of death? Why or why not?

What does death mean to you?

Are you ready to die?

What were your last wishes and final disposition of your possessions?

Imagine yourself in your coffin.

Who has attended your wake and funeral?

What are they saying about you?

Who will remember and pray for you after you die?

Is there anything you would have hoped to do while alive but hadn't as of yet?

What kind of life would you have wanted to live?

What would you say to Christ when you stand before Him in judgment?

What do you believe He would say to you?

What preparations should you make to prepare you for death?

If you died right now, would you be appropriately spiritually prepared?

How would you best use the time allotted to you before your death?

Awake and refresh yourself and remember, "Eternity begins here and now."

■   Ask Christ to fill your heart with a love for Him.

Ask Him to help you to remain detached from earthly glories. Ask Him for forgiveness and for the grace to forgive others. Ask Him for the courage to remain faithful even until the last moment. Ask St. Joseph, the patron of a happy death, for his prayers to persevere in life. Ask the Blessed Virgin Mother for her prayers to help you love unconditionally and to emulate her humility.

■ Say the following prayers slowly and reverentially. Allow them to speak to your heart.[9]

Miserere (Psalm 51)

Have mercy on me, God, in your kindness. In your compassion blot out my offense. O wash me more and more from my guilt and cleanse me from my sin. My offenses truly I know them; my sin is always before me. Against you, you alone, have I sinned; what is evil in your sight I have done. That you may be justified when you give sentence and be without reproach when you judge. O see, in guilt was I born, a sinner was I conceived. Indeed you love truth in the heart; then in the secret of my heart teach me wisdom. O purify me, then I shall be clean; O wash me, I shall be whiter than snow. Make me hear rejoicing and gladness that the bones you have crushed may revive. From my sins turn away your face and blot out all my guilt. A pure heart create for me, O God, put a steadfast spirit within me. Do not cast me away from your presence, nor deprive me of your holy spirit. Give me again the joy of your help; with a spirit of fervor sustain me, that I may teach transgressors your ways and sinners may return to you. O rescue me, God, my helper, and my tongue shall ring out your goodness. O Lord, open my lips and my mouth shall declare your praise. For in sacrifice you take no delight, burnt offering from me you would refuse; my sacrifice, a contrite spirit. A humbled, contrite heart you will not spurn. In your goodness, show favor to Zion: rebuild the walls of Jerusalem. Then you will be pleased with lawful sacrifice, holocausts offered on your altar.

De Profundis (Psalm 130)

Out of the depths I cry to you, O Lord;

Lord, hear my voice!

Let your ears be attentive

to my voice in supplication:

If you, O Lord, mark iniquities,

Lord, who can stand?

But with you is forgiveness,

that you may be revered.

I trust in the Lord;

my soul trusts in his word.

My soul waits for the Lord

more than sentinels wait for the dawn.

More than sentinels wait for the dawn,

let Israel wait for the Lord.

For with the Lord is kindness,

and with him is plenteous redemption;

And he will redeem Israel

from all their iniquities.

■ Appreciate your death.

Death defines us as mortal beings whose existence is completely dependent upon the Creator. We can die at any time, possibly today—we must be prepared. Put your suffering and that of others in its proper perspective. Remember that Christ suffered an ignominious death and continues to suffer because of our thoughtlessness.

✖ SCRIPTURE READING

Now that we have been put right with God through faith, we have peace with God through our Lord Jesus Christ. He has brought us by faith into this experience of God's grace, in which we now live.

And so we boast of the hope we have of sharing God's glory! We also boast of our troubles, because we know that trouble produces endurance, endurance brings God's approval, and his approval creates hope. This hope does not disappoint us, for God has poured out his love into our hearts by means of the Holy Spirit, who is God's gift to us. For when we were still helpless, Christ died for the wicked at the time that God chose. It is a difficult thing for someone to die for a righteous person. It may even be that someone might dare to die for a good person. But God has shown us how much he loves us—it was while we were still sinners that Christ died for us! By his blood we are now put right with God; how much more, then, will we be saved by him from God's anger! We were God's enemies, but he made us his friends through the death of his Son. Now that we are God's friends, how much more will we be saved by Christ's life! But that is not all; we rejoice because of what God has done through our Lord Jesus Christ, who has now made us God's friends. Sin came into the world through one man, and his sin brought death with it. As a result, death has spread to the whole human race because everyone has sinned. There was sin in the world before the Law was given; but where there is no law, no account is kept of sins. But from the time of Adam to the time of Moses, death ruled over all human beings, even over those who did not sin in the same way that Adam did when he disobeyed God's command. Adam was a figure of the one who was to come. But the two are not the same, because God's free gift is not like Adam's sin. It is true that many people died because of the sin of that one man. But God's grace is much greater, and so is his free gift to so many people through the grace of the one man, Jesus Christ. And there is a difference between God's gift and the sin of one man. After the one sin, came the judgment of Guilty; but after so many sins, comes the undeserved gift of Not guilty!

(Rom. 5:1–16)

Contemplating upon the Crucifix and Genuflecting

Then Jesus said to his disciples,
"If any of you want to come with me,
you must forget yourself, carry your cross, and follow me.
For if you want to save your own life, you will lose it; but
if you lose your life for my sake, you will find it."

—MATTHEW 16:24–25

❖ STRUCTURE OF PRAYER

Dominic would combine the acts of adoring and contemplating the crucifix and genuflecting, a traditional physical response to such adoration. He often used this form of prayer whenever he could steal away for private prayer. While contemplating the cross on the wall or in his hands, Dominic would pour his entire self out to Jesus. The act of genuflecting is a humbling action in and of itself. One naturally looks upward as if begging, which is quite appropriate considering to Whom we are praying. It is a highly intimate and personal form of worship.

✠ HOW TO PRACTICE

- Sit or stand before a crucifix or keep one in your hands.

- Genuflect as you regard the Crucified One and contemplate His Passion and sacrifice.

Dominic would use this form of prayer well into night just before retiring, but, of course, you may use it at any time during the day, genuflecting continually.

- Keep in mind the story of the leper who approached Christ and begged to be healed.

When Jesus came down from the hill, large crowds followed him. Then a man suffering from a dreaded skin disease came to him, knelt down before him, and said, "Sir, if you want to, you can make me clean." Jesus reached out and touched him. "I do want to," he answered. "Be clean!" At once the man was healed of his disease. (Matt. 8:1–3)

- Remember the leper's words: "Sir, if you want to, you can make me clean" (Matt. 8:2). These are powerful words. Recall the leper knelt before the Lord to beseech Him.

- Recall that when St. Stephen, the first martyr, was being stoned to death, he knelt before his tormentors and prayed for them, saying: "'Lord! Do not remember this sin against them!' He said this and died" (Acts 7:60).

You will find that while using this prayer form, you will start to have a palpable feeling of becoming more confident in God's mercy toward you and a greater confidence in God's plan for the world and for humanity. If you feel called to silence in the midst of this prayer form, that is perfectly acceptable, but also feel free to speak your heart aloud to the Object of Your Desire. He awaits you and longs for your company as you do for His.

According to the *Nine Ways*, it was not uncommon in these intense periods of prayer for a person to be given to joyous tears and even a type of spiritual excitement. When Dominic prayed in this manner, he was said to appear as if "longing and in anticipation like a thirsty man who has reached a spring, and like a traveler who is at last approaching his homeland."[10]

The Stations of the Cross

When they came to the place called "The Skull," they crucified Jesus there. (Lk. 23:33)

The Stations of the Cross, or Via Dolorosa, were developed as a result of those Christians who were incapable of going on costly pilgrimages to Jerusalem, Canterbury, Rome, or Santiago de Compostela in northern Spain. They would erect stations in their gardens to meditate upon the sufferings of the Lord. It is an excellent means by which to remind oneself of Christ's Passion and what He did for us. The Stations of the Cross are generally used as a community prayer, but they can easily be adapted as a private devotion. Consider the following prayer form in your own devotions.

- Continue your meditation, before the crucifix, with the Act of Contrition.

O my God, I am heartily sorry for having offended you, and I detest all my sins, because of Your just punishments, but most of all because they offend You, my God, who are all-good and deserving of all my love. I firmly resolve, with the help of Your grace, to sin no more and to avoid the near occasion of sin.

- Concentrate upon each station. Place yourself in the scene. What do you see? Who is around you? Where is Jesus? How do you interact with Him?

- Respond silently with your own prayer. Allow the above scene to take up space in your heart. Allow your gratitude to express itself to your Savior.

- At the beginning of each station, pray the following prayer: "We adore You, O Christ, and we bless You. Because by Your holy cross You have redeemed the world." Recite the Our Father, the Hail Mary, and the Glory Be prayers. Then pray, "Jesus Christ Crucified, have mercy on us. May the souls of the faithful departed, through the mercy of God, rest in peace. Amen."

Move on to the next Station of the Cross until you've finished all sixteen of them.

1 Jesus is condemned to death

2 Jesus carries His cross

3 Jesus falls for the first time

4 Jesus meets His mother

5 Simon helps Jesus carry His cross

6 Veronica wipes the face of Jesus[11]

7 Jesus falls the second time

The Passion of the Christ

When Jesus was sentenced to death in AD 33, the Roman pagans had designed crucifixion to be the worst possible form of torture and execution. They were experts at it, having already killed countless others using this method.

Jesus was first sentenced to forty lashes. The torture was so severe that it literally tore the skin from His body. After being beaten nearly to death, He was crowned with painful thorns that were approximately three inches long and dug deep into His skull. He was then forced to march the distance between Pontius Pilate's palace and the place of His execution, about a mile, carrying the heavy crossbar of the cross upon which He would be crucified. It weighed about fifty pounds. He was in such a pained and sorrowful condition, He needed the help of Simon of Cyrene, an innocent bystander, to get Him to Golgotha.

It was not only an excruciating and horrific punishment but it was also designed to be humiliating to the prisoner, so most likely Christ was naked when He was crucified.

Only the worst criminals were condemned to be crucified. Imagine how much worse it was for Jesus considering He was innocent of the charges the Temple Sanhedrin levied against Him. Instead, those Temple authorities begged the Roman authorities to crucify Him because they were upset at Christ's moral and spiritual authority, which usurped their own power.

Each of the nails that pierced His hands and feet was six to eight inches long. Two of the nails were driven through His wrists. To set His body properly upon His cross, most likely the Roman executioners nailed one of His hands into the cross and then viciously pulled His other arm, dislocating His shoulder, to properly align His other hand on the other side of the cross.

Both of His feet were nailed together. Thus Jesus had to support His entire weight upon the single nail, adding to the pain He suffered. Being stretched across His cross in such a way, Jesus couldn't breathe easily. He had to lift Himself upon the single nail that impaled His feet in order to take a breath. Jesus endured this extraordinary pain for three hours in the blazing sun without water. He died of asphyxiation, exhaustion, dehydration, and exsanguination (blood loss).

- As you remain before the crucifix, imagine what His Passion must have been like.

Christ died for you so that your sins could be washed away. He died for you. He died for His believers. He died for those who refuse to believe in Him. He died for those who died long before He ever incarnated into this world. He died for everyone who will be born in the future.

- Imagine what His Love must be like.

Christ's Passion upon the cross is unimaginable in its cruelty. But, without it, the world and everyone in it would have been doomed. Consider the suffering of the world in the light of Christ's Passion and in your own life.

Then Pilate set Barabbas free for them; and after he had Jesus whipped, he handed him over to be crucified. Then Pilate's soldiers took Jesus into the governor's palace, and the whole company gathered around him. They stripped off his clothes and put a scarlet robe on him. Then they made a crown out of thorny branches and placed it on his head, and put a stick in his right hand; then they knelt before him and made fun of him. "Long live the King of the Jews!" they said. They spat on him, and took the stick and hit him over the head. When they had finished making fun of him, they took the robe off and put his own clothes back on him. Then they led him out to crucify him. As they were going out, they met a man from Cyrene named Simon, and the soldiers forced him to carry Jesus' cross. They came to a place called Golgotha, which means, "The Place of the Skull." There they offered Jesus wine mixed with a bitter substance; but after tasting it, he would not drink it. They crucified him and then divided his clothes among them by throwing dice. After that they sat there and watched him. Above his head they put the written notice of the accusation against him: "This is Jesus, the King of the Jews." Then they crucified two bandits with Jesus, one on his right and the other on his left. People passing by shook their heads and hurled insults at Jesus: "You were going to tear down the Temple and build it back up in three days! Save yourself if you are God's Son! Come on down from the cross!" In the same way the chief priests and the teachers of the Law and the elders made fun of him: "He saved others, but he cannot save himself! Isn't he the king of Israel? If he will come down off the cross now, we will believe in him! He trusts in God and claims to be God's Son. Well, then, let us see if God wants to save him now!" Even the bandits who had been crucified with him insulted him in the same way. At noon the whole country was covered with darkness, which lasted for three hours. At about three o'clock Jesus cried out with a loud shout, "Eli, Eli, lema sabachthani?" which means, "My God, my God, why did you abandon me?" Some of the people standing there heard him and said, "He is calling for Elijah!" One of them ran up at once, took a sponge, soaked it in cheap wine, put it on the end of a stick, and tried to make him drink it. But the others said, "Wait, let us see if Elijah is coming to save him!" Jesus again gave a loud cry and breathed his last.

(Matt. 27:26–50)

Standing Before God

"I am Gabriel," the angel answered. "I stand in the
presence of God, who sent me to speak to you and tell
you this good news."

—LUKE 1:19

▚ STRUCTURE OF PRAYER

St. Dominic would stand before Christ's altar without leaning on anything
and allow his body to respond to what he experienced in prayer. At first
glance, this simple form of prayer may seem like nothing remarkable. But
for Dominic, and for those who experiment with it, it can be highly and
spiritually productive.

The saint would become so moved by this prayer form that he would
come to tears and clap his hands over his eyes both in joy and in sorrow.
At other times, he would raise his hands up to shoulder height as would a
presider (celebrant) at Mass. In still other times, he would hold his hands
outward as if holding an open book. He would stand with great reverence

and devotion, and often he would be heard repeating Holy Scriptures in soft, sweet tones, having been moved to do so by the Holy Spirit.

✖ HOW TO PRACTICE

- Stand before Christ's altar (or an icon) with your arms stretched out before you, palms upward, standing erect without supporting yourself or leaning upon anything.

- Recall that you stand before God. Recall His overwhelming love for you and for all humanity and for all creation.

- Pray the following prayers reverentially.

Lord, I look up to you, up to heaven, where you rule. As a servant depends on his master, as a maid depends on her mistress, so we will keep looking to you, O Lord our God, until you have mercy on us.
(Ps. 123:1–2)

God is powerful; all must stand in awe of him; he keeps his heavenly kingdom in peace.
(Job 25:1)

One day spent in your Temple is better than a thousand anywhere else; I would rather stand at the gate of the house of my God than live in the homes of the wicked.

(Ps. 84:10)

Praise the Lord! Praise his name, you servants of the Lord, who stand in the Lord's house, in the Temple of our God. Praise the Lord, because he is good; sing praises to his name, because he is kind.

(Ps. 135:1–3)

"Stop fighting," he says, "and know that I am God, supreme among the nations, supreme over the world."

(Ps. 46:10)

We always stand before God every second of our lives—not just when we are at Mass and receiving the sacraments. And when we die, we will stand before God in judgment. Let this sobering thought rest in your heart and soul.

✠ SCRIPTURE READING

When the Son of Man comes as King and all the angels with him, he will sit on his royal throne, and the people of all the nations will be gathered before him. Then he will divide them into two groups, just as a shepherd separates the sheep from the goats. He will put the righteous people at his right and the others at his left. Then the King will say to the people on his right, "Come, you that are blessed by my Father! Come and possess the kingdom which has been prepared for you ever since the creation of the world. I was hungry and you fed me, thirsty and you gave me a drink; I was a stranger and you received me in your homes, naked and you clothed me; I was sick and you took care of me, in prison and you visited me." The righteous will then answer him, "When, Lord, did we ever see you hungry and feed you, or thirsty and give you a drink? When did we ever see you a stranger and welcome you in our homes, or naked and clothe you? When did we ever see you sick or in prison, and visit you?" The King will reply, "I tell you, whenever you did this for one of the least important of these followers of mine, you did it for me!" Then he will say to those on his left, "Away from me, you that are under God's curse! Away to the eternal fire which has been prepared for the Devil and his angels! I was hungry but you would not feed me, thirsty but you would not give me a drink; I was a stranger but you would not welcome me in your homes, naked but you would not clothe

me; I was sick and in prison but you would not take care of me."
Then they will answer him, "When, Lord, did we ever see you
hungry or thirsty or a stranger or naked or sick or in prison, and
we would not help you?" The King will reply, "I tell you, whenever
you refused to help one of these least important ones, you refused
to help me." These, then, will be sent off to eternal punishment,
but the righteous will go to eternal life.

(Matt. 25:31–46)

Standing in the Cruciform Position, Contemplating Christ's Passion and Death and Praying the Rosary

The Rosary of Mary is the principle and foundation on which the very Order of Saint Dominic rests for making perfect the life of its members and obtaining the salvation of others.

—POPE PIUS XI

✖ STRUCTURE OF PRAYER

Dominic was often seen praying while standing erect with his hands and arms outstretched forcefully in the form of a cross. It is said that he would radiate holiness when he prayed the Rosary while standing in this cruciform shape. *The Nine Ways of Prayer* points out that Dominic would "shine with the spiritual insight of David, the ardor of Elias, the charity of

*Standing
in the
Cruciform
Position,
Contemplating
Christ's Passion
and Death*

78

Christ."[12] He may have held a set of rosary beads in one of his hands as he prayed, but it is at least as likely that he had the order and number of prayers committed to memory.

The saint would not use this sixth form of prayer as a planned activity. Rather, he would wait until he was inspired by God to pray this way. Although Dominic did not forbid his friars and nuns to pray in the cruciform manner, he didn't encourage them to do so. However, when his friars and nuns or sisters witnessed him praying in the cruciform position, they were fascinated by this most unusual and astonishing way of communicating with God. It inspired in them a great sense of awe and reverence. It is also said by these witnesses that many extraordinary miracles were attributed to Dominic when he prayed in this manner.

✖ HOW TO PRACTICE

■ Begin by reading the following Scriptural passages.

Hear my prayer; listen to my cry for help! So many troubles have fallen on me that I am close to death. I am like all others who are about to die; all my strength is gone. I am abandoned among the dead; I am like the slain lying in their graves, those you have forgotten completely, who are beyond your help. You have thrown me into the depths of the tomb, into the darkest and deepest pit. Your anger lies heavy on me, and I am crushed beneath its waves. You have caused my friends to abandon me; you have made me repulsive to them. I am closed in and cannot escape; my eyes are weak from suffering. Lord, every day I call to you and lift my hands to you in prayer. Do you perform miracles for the dead? Do they rise up and praise you?

(Ps. 88:2–10)

Lord, hear my prayer! In your righteousness listen to my plea; answer me in your faithfulness! Don't put me, your servant, on trial; no one is innocent in your sight. My enemies have hunted me down and completely defeated me. They have put me in a dark prison, and I am like those who died long ago. So I am ready to give up; I am in deep despair. I remember the days gone by; I think about all that you have done, I bring to mind all your deeds. I lift up my hands to you in prayer; like dry ground my soul is thirsty for you. Answer me now, Lord! I have lost all hope. Don't hide yourself from me, or I will be among those who go down to the world of the dead.

(Ps. 143:1–7)

- Next, stretch out your arms as Christ did upon the cross and close your eyes.

- With your eyes shut, feel the positioning of your limbs.

- Pray the Rosary starting with the Five Sorrowful Mysteries.

You may keep the rosary beads in your hand as your arms are extended in the shape of the cross. If you are completely familiar with the order of prayers used in the Rosary, you may simply count them off on your fingers.

About the Rosary

[The Rosary] sets forth the mystery of Christ in the very way in which it is seen by St. Paul in the celebrated "hymn" of the Epistle to the Philippians—kenosis,[13] death, and exaltation (2:6–11). . . . By its nature the recitation of the Rosary calls for a quiet rhythm and a lingering pace, helping the individual to meditate on the mysteries of the Lord's life as grasped by the heart of her who was closer to the Lord than all others.

—Pope Paul VI, Devotion to the Blessed Virgin Mary

Legend tells us that St. Dominic preached the Rosary inspired by a vision of the Blessed Virgin Mother. The use of 150 Hail Mary prayers had been popular for many years prior to St. Dominic's birth, but the systemization of praying the Rosary as we know it today was probably created by him.

Whether or not he actually received the Rosary directly from the hands of the Blessed Virgin Mary, Dominic and his Order of Preachers certainly popularized the prayer form. The Rosary is a common faith community, family, and individual prayer used by Catholics, Anglicans, and Lutherans. This prayer has sustained more Christians over the years than perhaps any other in history.

About the number of prayers: The Rosary should be seen more as a timing mechanism for prayer rather than a counting device, as there is no special mystical significance to the number of prayers (150)—except that there are the same number of psalms in the Bible. That is, the key to the Rosary is to rest in God's presence and not to "get through" as many prayers as possible.

Our Father
Glory Be . . .
Decade of Ten Hail Marys

Our Father
Glory Be . . .

Decade of Ten Hail Marys

Decade of Ten Hail Marys

Glory Be . . .
Our Father

Decade of Ten Hail Marys

Our Father
Glory Be . . .

Decade of Ten Hail Marys

Glory Be . . .
(End with Hail, Holy Queen)

Our Father

Glory Be . . .

3 Hail Marys
Our Father

Apostles' Creed
(Start)

The Rosary facilitates the meditation of twenty key mysteries of Christ's life and, at the same time, a devotion to the Blessed Virgin Mother. The word *rosary* is derived from the Latin word *rosarium,* meaning "rose garden." Throughout Scriptures and Church tradition, Mary is associated with roses, thus the connection with the Rosary. It can be used as oral prayer, as part of one's silent meditation, or as an aid for contemplation. Even without a set of rosary beads, one can still pray the Rosary simply by using one's fingers. In fact, Giuseppe Rivella, a waiter in a Roman restaurant, counted the heads of his customers who sat in groups of ten at the tables he waited upon. Every ten patrons constituted a decade of the Rosary. When he died, Vatican Radio announced: "A holy man has died in Rome."[14]

The Rosary starts off with reciting the Apostle's Creed, followed by an Our Father, three Hail Marys, and one Glory Be. This is followed by fifty Hail Marys in groups of ten, each referred to as a "decade." Each decade is preceded by an Our Father and capped off with a Glory Be and a Fatima Prayer (see below).[15]

Prior to Dominic's popularization of the Rosary, the 150 psalms in Scripture were widely used in the Liturgy of the Hours, said or sung every day by monks, priests, brothers, nuns, religious sisters, and lay people around the world. St. Eligius, seventh-century Bishop of Noyon-Tournai, prayed 150 Hail Marys of the Psalter of Mary and used a proto-rosary to keep track of them. Ninth-century Irish monks replaced the 150 psalms with Our Fathers for illiterate Christians who hoped to emulate the monks' holiness. Eventually, the Hail Marys came to replace the Our Fathers as the prayer most associated with the devotion. The twelfth-century English anchorites' monastic Rule known as the *Ancrene Wisse* (Guide for Anchoresses) specified how groups of 50 Hail Marys were to be broken into five sets of ten prayers each.[16] Eventually, each decade came to be preceded by an Our Father. In the thirteenth century, Dominic of Prussia

(1382–1460), a Carthusian mystic, associated with the Rosary meditations on Christ's life—specifically, His ministry, death, and resurrection—and the life of His mother. He referred to the prayer as the "Life of Jesus Rosary," and it became formalized and dedicated as a meditative practice recognizable as the Rosary that contemporary Christians recite.[17] The Rosary soon became popular among Carthusian and Benedictine monks. In the Blessed Virgin's apparitions at Lourdes in France (1858) and Fatima in Portugal (1917), Mary encouraged the faithful to pray the Rosary. In fact, an additional prayer (the Fatima Prayer) was added because she requested it:

O my Jesus, forgive us our sins, save us from the fires of hell. Lead all souls to heaven, especially those who have most need of your mercy. Amen.

Although some nonbelievers, and even some Catholics, might think the Rosary to be quaint and outdated, the truth is that the gentle repetition of simple prayers is comforting and sure to calm the hyperactive mind and soothe the troubled soul. While praying the Rosary, the individual feels the sensation that the Rosary is praying him and, in this passive, receptive mode, the Holy Spirit imbues the individual with love, peace, faith, and hope, the very essentials of life.

St. Louis de Montfort, an eighteenth-century French Dominican Tertiary, was particularly devoted to the Rosary. Among his admonitions, he warned against mechanistic, repetitive prayer. This is not to say one must struggle to constantly produce uniquely worded prayer. Repeating prayers like the Hail Mary and the Our Father are perfectly acceptable provided one doesn't repeat them unthinkingly. In his book *The Secret of the Rosary*, one of the best books ever written on the subject, St. Louis de Montfort emphasized the importance of being pure in our intention— otherwise we risk the possibility of attempting to be manipulative, in which case we aren't practicing spirituality at all but rather a ritualistic magic. He also pressed the importance of the proper spiritual attitude and mental preparation before and during prayer.[18] We would naturally be reverent and respectful of our grandparents or a friend, spouse, or our children. It follows that in prayer when we meet our Creator, He Who brought us out of chaos and into His Light, surely we should meet Him reverently.[19]

Christ's life, Passion, Crucifixion, and Resurrection were meant to heal all. The Rosary guides us in the remembrance of key points of His ministry. All of our faith is distilled into this tiny handful of beads. Keep it close to you and you will come to understand the mysteries of Christ's life.

✖ SCRIPTURE PASSAGE

Moses said to Joshua, "Pick out some men to go and fight the Amalekites tomorrow. I will stand on top of the hill holding the stick that God told me to carry." Joshua did as Moses commanded him and went out to fight the Amalekites, while Moses, Aaron, and Hur went up to the top of the hill. As long as Moses held up his arms, the Israelites won, but when he put his arms down, the Amalekites started winning. When Moses' arms grew tired, Aaron and Hur brought a stone for him to sit on, while they stood beside him and held up his arms, holding them steady until the sun went down. In this way Joshua totally defeated the Amalekites. Then the Lord said to Moses, "Write an account of this victory, so that it will be remembered. Tell Joshua that I will completely destroy the Amalekites." Moses built an altar and named it "The Lord is my Banner." He said, "Hold high the banner of the Lord! The Lord will continue to fight against the Amalekites forever!" (Exod. 17:9–16)

■ Pray the Mysteries of the Rosary according to the days of the week.

The Five Joyful Mysteries (Monday and Saturday)

MYSTERY	VIRTUE	SCRIPTURE	EXPLANATION
Annunciation	Humility	Luke 1:26–38	The Angel Gabriel appears to Mary telling her she is to become the Mother of God.
Visitation	Charity	Luke 1:39–56	Elizabeth greets Mary: "Blessed art thou among women and blessed is the fruit of thy womb!"
Nativity	Poverty/ Detachment from world	Luke 2:1–20	The Blessed Virgin Mary gives birth to the Savior of the World.
Presentation of Our Lord	Purity of Heart/ Obedience	Luke 2:22–39	Mary presents the Child Jesus in the Temple.
Finding of Our Lord in the Temple	Piety	Luke 2:42–52	The Blessed Mother finds Jesus in the Temple.

The Five Luminous Mysteries (Thursday)

MYSTERY	VIRTUE	SCRIPTURE	EXPLANATION
Baptism in the Jordan	Our personal commitment to God	John 1:29–34	God speaks at Christ's Baptism announcing that He is His beloved Son.
Wedding at Cana	Miracles in our lives	John 2:1–11	Christ's first miracle and the beginning of His ministry at His Mother's intervention and urging.
Announcement of the Kingdom	Hope for our future lives	Matthew 4:17	Jesus proclaims the coming of God's Kingdom and calls us all to conversion.
Transfiguration	Transformation in our lives	Matthew 17:1–8	Christ is transfigured and shines in His glory. The Father tells the amazed Apostles to "listen to Him."
Institution of the Eucharist	Food for our salvation	Matthew 26:26–30	Christ offers His Body and Blood as food under the signs of bread and wine and testifies His love for us, and our salvation He will offer Himself in sacrifice.

The Five Sorrowful Mysteries (Tuesday and Friday)

MYSTERY	VIRTUE	SCRIPTURE	EXPLANATION
Agony in the Garden	Contrition for our Sins	Luke 22:39–44	Jesus prays in the Garden of Gethsemane as He contemplates His fate and the sins of the world.
Scourging at the Pillar	Purity/ Mortification of our Senses	Matthew 27:26	Jesus is cruelly whipped, shedding His blood for Humanity.
Crowning with Thorns	Courage/ Interior mortification	Matthew 27:28–31	A crown of thorns is placed on Jesus's head.
Carrying of the Cross	Fortitude/ Patience under crosses	Luke 23:26–32	Jesus is made to carry His cross.
Crucifixion and Death of Our Lord	Self-Denial that we may die to ourselves	Matthew 27:33–50	Jesus is nailed to the cross and dies.

The Five Glorious Mysteries (Sunday and Wednesday)

MYSTERY	VIRTUE	SCRIPTURE	EXPLANATION
Resurrection	Faith, Conversion of Heart	Matthew 28:1–20	Jesus rises three days after His death, thus destroying Death forever.
Ascension	Hope, A desire for Heaven	Luke 24:50–51	Jesus ascends into Heaven forty days after His Resurrection.
Coming of the Holy Spirit	Love, The Gifts of the Holy Spirit	Acts 2:24	The Holy Spirit descends upon Mary and the Apostles.
Assumption of our Blessed Mother into heaven	Devotion to Mary	Revelation 12:12–17	The Blessed Mother is united once again with her Divine Son in Heaven.
Coronation of our Blessed Mother	Eternal Happiness	Revelation 12:1–2	Mary is crowned Queen of Heaven and earth.

More Prayers of the Rosary

Sign of the Cross

In the name of the Father and of the Son and of the Holy Spirit. Amen.

The Apostles' Creed

I believe in God, the Father almighty, Creator of heaven and earth, and in Jesus Christ, his only Son, our Lord, who was conceived by the Holy Spirit, born of the Virgin Mary, suffered under Pontius Pilate, was crucified, died, and was buried. He descended into hell; on the third day he rose again from the dead; he ascended into heaven, and sits at the right hand of God the Father almighty; from there he will come to judge the living and the dead. I believe in the Holy Spirit, the holy Catholic Church, the communion of saints, the forgiveness of sins, the resurrection of the body, and life everlasting. Amen.

Our Father

Our Father, who art in heaven, hallowed by Thy name; Thy kingdom come; Thy will be done on earth as it is in heaven. Give us this day our daily bread; and forgive us our trespasses as we forgive those who trespass against us; and lead us not into temptation, but deliver us from evil. For the kingdom, the power, and the glory are yours, now and forever. Amen.

Hail Mary

Hail Mary, full of grace, the Lord is with thee. Blessed art thou among women and blessed is the fruit of thy womb, Jesus. Holy Mary, Mother of God, pray for us sinners now and at the hour of our death. Amen.

Glory Be

Glory be to the Father, and to the Son, and to the Holy Spirit. As it was in the beginning, is now, and ever shall be, world without end. Amen.

O My Jesus (Our Lady of Fatima Prayer) (after each decade of the rosary)

O my Jesus, forgive us our sins, save us from the fires of hell.

Lead all souls to heaven, especially those who have most need of your mercy.

Salve Regina (Hail, Holy Queen) (after the complete rosary)

Hail, Holy Queen! Mother of Mercy, our life, our sweetness, and our hope! To thee do we cry, poor banished children of Eve; to thee do we send up our sighs, mourning and weeping in this valley of tears. Turn then, most gracious advocate, thine eyes of mercy toward us, and after this our exile, show unto us the blessed fruit of thy womb, Jesus. O clement, O loving, O sweet Virgin Mary!

℣. Pray for us, O Holy Mother of God,

℟. That we may be made worthy of the Promises of Christ.

Let us pray: O God, whose only begotten Son by his life, death, and resurrection has purchased for us rewards of everlasting life, grant, we beseech you, that meditating on these mysteries of the Most Holy Rosary of the Blessed Virgin Mary, we may imitate what they contain and obtain what they promise, through the same Christ Our Lord. Amen.

Praying with Hands Held High in Humble Supplication

> A man who governs his passions is master of the world. We must either command them, or be enslaved by them. It is better to be a hammer than an anvil.
>
> —St. Dominic

❖ STRUCTURE OF PRAYER

In the seventh form of prayer, Dominic would pray with his hands outstretched above his head and joined together, or at times slightly separated as if about to receive something from heaven. In this position, the saint gave the impression that he was receiving God's grace in the form of gifts of the Holy Spirit.

While praying in this manner he always sought—for himself and for his friars and nuns—the transcendent joy that is found in living the Beatitudes, the Ten Commandments, and the Evangelical Counsels (i.e., obedience, poverty, and chasitity). The fruits of this prayer form were apparent to everyone who knew Dominic. They and he were convinced that each considered himself or herself truly blessed even if they found themselves in extreme poverty, or in mourning, or in the midst of unjust persecutions.

Dominic would not remain at this type of prayer for long periods of time. It is said that after practicing this form, Dominic seemed to be imbued with the Holy Spirit's peace and love and assured of his ministry. It is little wonder that he was so successful in preaching against the heretical Albigensians.

⧉ HOW TO PRACTICE

- Say the following prayer aloud in a clear voice or in the quietness of your heart.

  Hear me when I cry to you for help, when I lift my hands toward your holy Temple.
  (Ps. 28:2)

- Stretch out your hands above your head and join them together as in prayer. Say the following scriptural passage either silently or aloud.

  Come, praise the Lord, all his servants, all who serve in his Temple at night. Raise your hands in prayer in the Temple, and praise the

Lord! May the Lord, who made heaven and earth, bless you from Zion!

(Ps. 134:1–3)

Now, open your arms, separating them as if to receive a great gift from God. Say the following scriptural passage either silently or aloud.

I call to you, Lord; help me now! Listen to me when I call to you. Receive my prayer as incense, my uplifted hands as an evening sacrifice.

(Ps. 141:1–2)

■ Consider the many gifts you have received from the Lord of All and express your thankfulness to Him for them.

■ Consider the Ten Commandments that God gave to Moses on Mt. Sinai.

"I am the Lord your God, Who brought you out of the land of Egypt, out of the house of slavery; you shall have no other gods before me. You shall not make for yourself an idol, whether in the form of anything that is in heaven above, or that is on the earth beneath, or that is in the water under the earth. You shall not bow down to them or worship them; for I the LORD your God am a jealous God, punishing children for the iniquity of parents, to the third and fourth generation of those who reject me, but showing steadfast love to the thousandth generation of those who love me and keep my commandments.

"You shall not make wrongful use of the name of the LORD your God, for the LORD will not acquit anyone who misuses his name.

"Remember the sabbath day and keep it holy. Six days you shall labor and do all your work. But the seventh day is a sabbath to the LORD your God; you shall not do any work—you, your son or your daughter, your male or female slave, your livestock, or the alien resident in your towns. For in six days the LORD made heaven and earth, the sea, and all that is in them, but rested the seventh day; therefore the LORD blessed the sabbath day and consecrated it.

"Honor your father and your mother, so that your days may be long in the land that the LORD your God is giving you. You shall not murder. You shall not commit adultery. You shall not steal. You shall not bear false witness against your neighbor. You shall not covet your neighbor's house; you shall not covet your neighbor's wife, or male or female slave, or ox, or donkey, or anything that belongs to your neighbor."

(Exod. 20:1–17, NRSV)

■ Commit yourself to accept God's will in your life.

Consider the Beatitudes Jesus spoke upon Mount Karn Hattin (known as the Sermon on the Mount).

Blessed are the poor in spirit, for theirs is the kingdom of heaven.

Blessed are those who mourn, for they will be comforted.

Blessed are the meek, for they will inherit the earth.

Blessed are those that hunger and thirst for righteousness, for
they will be filled.

Blessed are the merciful, for they will receive mercy.

Blessed are the pure in heart, for they will see God.

Blessed are the peacemakers, for they will be called children
of God.

Blessed are those that are persecuted for righteousness' sake,
for theirs is the kingdom of heaven.

(Matt. 5:3–10, NRSV)

Use this prayer form to call upon God even in the worst of your trials. Invite Him to be always with you, especially during hard times. Be grateful for the great gift of your faith. Promise the Lord of All to strive to be worthy of it. Consider the Evangelical Counsels, also called "counsels of perfection" as described in Scriptures: chastity, poverty, obedience.

■ Allow God's love to fill your soul. Allow it to inspire you to live His Commandments, the Beatitudes, and the Evangelical Counsels.

■ Rest in the peace and love of the Holy Spirit.

■ Ask the Spirit of Life for the gifts to sustain you. Dedicate them to the service of others. Practice the Beatitudes in your everyday life. Let the Ten Commandments be your guide to life.

✦ SCRIPTURE READING

Jesus saw the crowds and went up a hill, where he sat down. His disciples gathered around him and he began to teach them: "Happy are those who know they are spiritually poor; the Kingdom of heaven belongs to them! Happy are those who mourn; God will comfort them! Happy are those who are humble; they will receive what God has promised! Happy are those whose greatest desire is to do what God requires; God will satisfy them fully! Happy are those who are merciful to others; God will be merciful to them! Happy are the pure in heart; they will see God! Happy are those who work for peace; God will call them his children! Happy are those who are persecuted because they do what God requires; the Kingdom of heaven belongs to them! Happy are you when people insult you and persecute you and tell all kinds of evil lies against you because you are my followers. Be happy and glad, for a great reward is kept for you in heaven. This is how the prophets who lived before you were persecuted. You are like salt for the whole human race. But if salt loses its saltiness, there is no way to make it salty again. It has become worthless, so it is thrown out and people trample on it. You are like light for the whole world. A city built on a hill cannot be hid. No one lights a lamp and puts it under a bowl;

Praying with
Hands Held
High in
Humble
Supplication

100

instead it is put on the lampstand, where it gives light for everyone in the house. In the same way your light must shine before people, so that they will see the good things you do and praise your Father in heaven.

(Matt. 5:1–16)

Spiritual Reading

Then Jesus went to Nazareth, where he had been brought up, and on the Sabbath he went as usual to the synagogue. He stood up to read the Scriptures and was handed the book of the prophet Isaiah. He unrolled the scroll and found the place where it is written, "The Spirit of the Lord is upon me, because he has chosen me to bring good news to the poor. He has sent me to proclaim liberty to the captives and recovery of sight to the blind, to set free the oppressed and announce that the time has come when the Lord will save his people." Jesus rolled up the scroll, gave it back to the attendant, and sat down. All the people in the synagogue had their eyes fixed on him, as he said to them, "This passage of scripture has come true today, as you heard it being read."

—Luke 4:16–21

*Praying with
Hands Held
High in
Humble
Supplication*

102

Dominic's eighth way of prayer was dedicated to reading either the Bible, especially the Gospels, or a spiritual treatise. When he practiced lectio divina, the reading of spiritual topics with spiritual intentions, he would do so alone, away from others. Before opening the book, he would make the sign of the cross and then give thanks to God for the book itself, his literacy, and the opportunity to read the book before him. He would lift it above his head and offer his thanks, then bring it to his lips and kiss it. When reading the Gospels, he would cross himself upon his forehead, his lips, and once again upon his heart as believers do during Mass when the Gospel is read aloud. He took special care and reverence when he read Christ's very words. When doing so, he would cover his head and hide his face with the hood of his habit. At times he was brought to tears of joy and repentance.

As Dominic read, he would focus intently on the text before him, making sure he engaged not only his faith but also his mind in deciding whether everything he read was appropriate and understandable. And, when he read a passage that was particularly moving, he would strike his breast, as Christians do during Mass, saying, "Mea culpa! Mea culpa! Mea maxima culpa!" ("Through my fault. Through my fault. Through my most grievous fault." Or, literally, "I am responsible for my sins! I am responsible for my sins! I am very responsible for my sins!").

When reading, we should move seamlessly from reading to prayer, from prayer to meditation, and from meditation to contemplation. After reading for a bit, Dominic would rise reverently and bow his head for a short time, offering a pray of thanksgiving. Wholly refreshed and in great interior peace, he then returned to his book.

St. Jerome (c. 347–420) is best known for having translated the Latin Vulgate Bible and for being a world-class curmudgeon, but most people wouldn't necessarily associate him with being an accomplished mystic. He reminded other Christians that "ignorance of Scripture is ignorance of Christ." He was so convinced of this that he took up Greek and Hebrew so that he could study Scripture in its original languages.

Reading Scripture is an important aid for a Christian's prayer, as one of our principal means of knowing God comes from the Bible. There are many ways one can ascertain God's will through prayerfully reading Scripture, including the Liturgy of the Word at the Eucharist and during the Liturgy of the Hours. Most major churches use a form of the Lectionary (the calendar of scriptural readings assigned to each day of the year), which can also be used for devotional purposes. If one attended a Catholic Mass every day for three years, one would have the entire Bible read to them. In addition, there are many commercially available "Bible-a-day" devotional books, which can lead Christians to a greater understanding of God. Spiritual reading can also be done through new technology, which makes available some reputable devotional websites and both modern and classic spiritual texts for e-book readers.

The first step to praying with Scripture is finding a quiet place, whether it is a chapel, a secluded outdoor spot, or any other peaceful, reflective space. Concentrate upon a small passage and consider the message, cultural elements, spiritual elements, and context. Consider the individuals in the passage and what they are asked to do. After reading or listening to a Scripture reading, select a word, phrase, concept, or parable that resonates with you. From there, follow the next three prayer steps, also known as the Trinitarian Model of Prayer.

1 Meditate (*meditatio*)—Select a single idea, whether it is a particular event, a parable, a miracle, a single scriptural passage, or a concept (for instance, God's love), and concentrate on it. Give yourself over to God and ask Him to lead your thoughts as He wishes. Let the meaning of the passage settle in your heart and allow it to transform you. How must you change your life to allow this transformation?

2 Pray (*oratio*)—Allow a prayer to form within your soul. Thank the Lord for His loving-kindness. Praise Him for His generosity.

Ask Him about your needs. How do you best respond to the scriptural passage? What does the passage say about you, your life, and your faith?

3   Contemplate (*contemplatio*)—Allow the Holy Spirit to silence your thoughts and still your soul. Rest in Him. Listen to what He tells you. Be receptive to God. Be content in His presence. Simply be.

Prayer for the Christian has never been a matter of sitting on a mountainside far removed from the suffering of humanity, just communing with nature. Even monks and cloistered nuns must interact with others from time to time, and even if they don't, as in the case of the Carthusians, they must remain lovingly attentive to their brothers in their monastic community. Prayer is meant to motivate the Christian to make a difference in our world, specifically in helping our fellow man. We could pray all day and it would make no difference in our lives unless we put food in the hands of the hungry, bring peace to the city in which we live, put clothes on the backs of the poor, and forgive our enemies. Anyone can appear in public with eyes closed and claim to be praying, but unless the result of that prayer is a deluge of overpowering love for all humanity, then the person is lying to both himself and others. Even in the case of cloistered nuns and monks, God's grace flows from them and prompts them to love each other and to pray for the entire world.

This Dominican prayer form has much in common with an important aspect of Ignatian spirituality. Father James Martin, SJ, author of *The Jesuit Guide to (Almost) Everything*, often lectures on this unique form of meditation that Jesuits learn during their religious formation.

You could call it imaginative prayer. In this method, you imagine yourself as part of a Scripture scene, using what you might call your "imaginative senses." So if you've chosen to pray with a scene where Jesus is preaching you may say, "What do I see?" "What do I hear?" "What do I smell?" "What do I feel physically?" You "compose" the place in your mind's eye, and then let the scene play out, with yourself as either an observer or a participant. Pay attention to what happens in your imagination, which is one of God's gifts to us, and so can be used as a way to meet him in a creative way. You might be surprised how deeply you enter into the scene. Scripture may come alive in new ways for you.[20]

As St. Jerome wrote, "There is no doubt that through the reading of the Sacred Scriptures the soul is set aflame in God and becomes purified from all vices." Scriptures are, in most cases, the initial introduction people have with Christ. By praying with the Scriptures we start a relationship of knowing God and inviting Him to know us. As you use this prayer form, remember St. Cyprian of Carthage's advice:

Be constantly committed to prayer or to reading [Scripture]; by praying, you speak to God; in reading, God speaks to you.

✖ HOW TO PRACTICE

- Select an appropriate passage or book to read.

- Retire to a quiet spot conducive to reading.

- Make the sign of the cross.

- Thank God for the book and for the opportunity to read it, praying that you will be illuminated by reading it, leading you to praise Jesus all the more.

- Say the following psalm: "I am listening to what the Lord God is saying" (Ps. 85:8).

- If reading the Gospels, cross yourself upon the forehead, lips, and heart as one does during Mass when the Gospel is read aloud, saying, "Lord, open my mind, my lips, and my heart to Your beauty. Help me understand."

Engage your reasoning skills when reading. God made you a rational, thinking person. You are allowed to question, wonder, and contemplate what you read. Feel free to take breaks, for example, after each chapter. When doing so, stand and bow your head as Dominic did, thanking God for the opportunity to gain in wisdom and understanding.

Christian Spiritual Bibliography

Thankfully, there is no end to literature that praises God and is meant to inspire Christians. Although the Bible, especially the four canonical Gospels, will always be the most important spiritual reading for Christians, there are many other books written by saints, mystics, and contemplatives that have inspired countless millions. In fact, I would be hard-pressed to find a saint who didn't read, let alone write, such books. Please consider reading some of the following titles. I've put them in alphabetical order by title.

Ascent of Mt. Carmel, St. John of the Cross

City of God, St. Augustine

Cleaving to God, St. Albert the Great

The Cloud of Unknowing, Anonymous

Confessions, St. Augustine

The Dark Night of the Soul, St. John of the Cross

Dialogues, St. Catherine of Siena

Great Means of Salvation and Perfection, St. Alphonsus de Liguori

Heart of Joy, Mother Teresa

A Holy Life, St. Bernadette of Lourdes

The Holy Rule of St. Benedict, St. Benedict

Imitation of Christ, Thomas à Kempis

The Interior Castle, St. Teresa of Ávila

Introduction to the Devout Life, St. Francis de Sales

Life Is Worth Living, Fulton J. Sheen

The Lion, the Witch, and the Wardrobe, C. S. Lewis

The Little Flowers of St. Francis of Assisi, Anonymous

The Lord of the Rings, J. R. R. Tolkien

Mere Christianity, C. S. Lewis

On Loving God, St. Bernard of Clairvaux

Orthodoxy, G. K. Chesterton

Poems of St. Thérèse, Carmelite of Lisieux, St. Thérèse of Lisieux

The Problem of Pain, C. S. Lewis

Revelations of Divine Love, Julian of Norwich

The Screwtape Letters, C. S. Lewis

The Seven Storey Mountain, Thomas Merton

The Soul's Journey into God, St. Bonaventure

Spiritual Exercises, St. Ignatius of Loyola

The Story of a Soul, St. Thérèse of Lisieux

Thirsting for God, Mother Teresa

Treatise on Purgatory, St. Catherine of Genoa

Treatise on the Love of God, St. Francis de Sales

True Devotion to the Blessed Virgin, St. Louis-Marie Grignion de Montfort

Let the words of the saints and mystics fill you. Learn from their wisdom. Be assured God has touched these authors in a special way for our own personal edification and enlightenment.

✖ SCRIPTURE READING

Listen to my words, O Lord, and hear my sighs. Listen to my cry for help, my God and king! I pray to you, O Lord; you hear my voice in the morning; at sunrise I offer my prayer and wait for your answer. You are not a God who is pleased with wrongdoing; you allow no evil in your presence. You cannot stand the sight of the proud; you hate all wicked people. You destroy all liars and despise violent, deceitful people. But because of your great love I can come into your house; I can worship in your holy Temple and bow down to you in reverence. Lord, I have so many enemies! Lead me to do your will; make your way plain for me to follow. What my enemies say can never be trusted; they only want to destroy. Their words are flattering and smooth, but full of deadly deceit. Condemn and punish them, O God; may their own plots cause their ruin. Drive them out of your presence because of their many sins and their rebellion against you. But all who find safety in you will rejoice; they can always sing for joy. Protect those who love you; because of you they are truly happy. You bless those who obey you, Lord; your love protects them like a shield.

(Ps. 5:1–12)

Meditation as Preparation to Contemplation

> At once the Spirit made him go into the desert, where he stayed forty days, being tempted by Satan. Wild animals were there also, but angels came and helped him.
>
> —Mark 1:12–13

❖ STRUCTURE OF PRAYER

Dominic often used this mode of prayer while traveling, especially through deserted areas. In those moments, he would gladly give himself over to meditation, which passed easily and effortlessly into contemplation (see the tenth way, below).

Dominic would sometimes sit in meditation, but he would also, at times, continue walking to do so. Throughout this form of prayer, he would cross himself repeatedly. And when he meditated, he was suffused with the fire of charity. It was through this prayer form—and the one that follows it—that Dominic came to understand God all the more.

The Nature of Meditation

Meditative prayer is simply a mental, that is, unspoken, prayer. It can include the Rosary, the Stations of the Cross, the sacraments, especially the Eucharist, *lectio divina*, and praying before icons, a crucifix, or the Holy Presence in the Eucharist. Journaling can be included as one rarely reads aloud that which one has written. Even praying with the newspaper and other visual media, such as television, is acceptable. In other words, this prayer form includes any way in which we pay close attention to world and local community events and bring them into our prayerful meditation.

⠶ HOW TO PRACTICE

- Find a quiet place, sit comfortably, and close your eyes.

- Make the sign of the cross.

- Pray the following: "Come, praise the Lord, all his servants, all who serve in his Temple at night. Raise your hands in prayer in the Temple, and praise the Lord! May the Lord, who made heaven and earth, bless you from Zion!" (Ps. 134:1–3).

- Breathe deeply and concentrate on your breathing.

■ Pray the following Scriptures.

O God, you are my God, and I long for you. My whole being
desires you; like a dry, worn-out, and waterless land, my soul is
thirsty for you. Let me see you in the sanctuary; let me see how
mighty and glorious you are. Your constant love is better than life
itself, and so I will praise you. I will give you thanks as long as I
live; I will raise my hands to you in prayer. My soul will feast and
be satisfied, and I will sing glad songs of praise to you. As I lie in
bed, I remember you; all night long I think of you, because you
have always been my help. In the shadow of your wings I sing for
joy. I cling to you, and your hand keeps me safe.
(Ps. 63:1–8)

Accept my prayer of thanks, O Lord, and teach me your commands.
I am always ready to risk my life; I have not forgotten your law.
(Ps. 119:108–9)

Quiet your mind by not thinking. If stray thoughts come to the
forefront, simply push them aside and return to your search for Christ.

Step by step, concentrate on relaxing every part of your body. Open yourself to God's love. Feel his presence. Trust in his faithfulness.

■ Now, imagine yourself alone in a forest. The sun brightly shines around you. Feel its warmth on your face and body. Next to you is a cave entrance. Step into it. Feel its cool air on your skin. Next to you are steps descending into the cool darkness. As you take each step down, you will see a large number 10 floating before you. With each step, the number will go down and you will feel calmer and more tranquil. When you get to 1, you will see a large, darkened cavern filled with water. Slowly step into it. You will note the water is invitingly warm.

As you move forward in the pool, the water is rising over your legs, torso, and neck. Submerge yourself in the warm, dark waters. You will find you can breathe underwater. Swim across the pool and slowly separate out of the pool. As your eyes focus, you notice Jesus standing on the edge of the pool beckoning you to join Him.

■ Embrace Jesus. Feel His love for you. Give your love to Him. Actively listen to Christ in your heart.

- Now, be open to how He moves you.

- When you are ready, thank Jesus for His love and your love.

- Then, reverse the above process and take leave of the underground cavern. Once you have reached the surface, open your eyes and pray the following.

I call to you, Lord; help me now! Listen to me when I call to you. Receive my prayer as incense, my uplifted hands as an evening sacrifice. Lord, place a guard at my mouth, a sentry at the door of my lips. Keep me from wanting to do wrong and from joining evil people in their wickedness. May I never take part in their feasts. Good people may punish me and rebuke me in kindness, but I will never accept honor from evil people, because I am always praying against their evil deeds.
(Ps. 141:1–5)

Allow your meditations to change your heart, soul, and mind. Empty yourself and allow God to speak to you, to form you, to guide you.

To you, O Lord, I offer my prayer; in you, my God, I trust. Save me from the shame of defeat; don't let my enemies gloat over me! Defeat does not come to those who trust in you, but to those who are quick to rebel against you. Teach me your ways, O Lord; make them known to me. Teach me to live according to your truth, for you are my God, who saves me. I always trust in you. Remember, O Lord, your kindness and constant love which you have shown from long ago. Forgive the sins and errors of my youth. In your constant love and goodness, remember me, Lord! Because the Lord is righteous and good, he teaches sinners the path they should follow. He leads the humble in the right way and teaches them his will. With faithfulness and love he leads all who keep his covenant and obey his commands. Keep your promise, Lord, and forgive my sins, for they are many. Those who have reverence for the Lord will learn from him the path they should follow. They will always be prosperous, and their children will possess the land. The Lord is the friend of those who obey him and he affirms his covenant with them. I look to the Lord for help at all times, and he rescues me from danger. Turn to me, Lord, and be merciful to me, because I am lonely and weak. Relieve me of my worries and save me from all my troubles. Consider my distress and suffering and forgive all my sins. See how many enemies I have; see how much they hate me. Protect me and save me; keep me from defeat. I come to you for safety. May my goodness and honesty preserve me, because I trust in you. From all their troubles, O God, save your people Israel!

(Ps. 25:1–22)

Ways to Meditate in the Midst of a Busy Life

Although in its strictest sense, meditation requires that one must simply sit, blocking out all external stimuli, it is also possible to meditate while actively doing something else, as long as that something else requires little concentration, such as walking, bicycling, washing the day's dishes, or weeding the garden. One's entire life should be dedicated to the Lord of All, not just the convenient quiet moments one snatches from an otherwise hectic schedule. In fact, Christian monasticism is specifically designed to rework one's day and, in fact, one's entire life to direct it better toward God—one's life is God-centered. Working, sleeping, and eating become secondary. In *The Way of a Pilgrim*, the author describes meeting a fellow Christian who prays the Jesus Prayer unceasingly even while eating and walking.

Pilgrimages and reading are also important opportunities to practice this meditative prayer form. We can often take time, while doing something else, to visualize God and can use any of the forms of prayer discussed in this book, or simply imagine a scene from Christ's life and place ourselves in it (for example, the Last Supper, at the Crucifixion, or the like).

Even more broadly understood, meditative prayer can incorporate "working prayer." Working prayer is dedicating our day's work, especially volunteering and works of charity, joyfully and honestly to the Lord. If we pray, our work can be prayer, but not if we don't. St. Francis, St. Ignatius Loyola, St. Thérèse of Lisieux, St. Josemaría Escrivá, and Servant of God Dorothy Day were all proponents of sacramentalizing our everyday lives for the greater glory of God. Many kinds of occasional work, too, such as cleaning up the environment, can be considered a working prayer if we do it to pay homage to God and for the sake of others. This form of prayer is also called the Illuminative Way.

Contemplation: The Perfect Prayer

Six days later Jesus took with him Peter and the brothers James and John and led them up a high mountain where they were alone. As they looked on, a change came over Jesus: his face was shining like the sun, and his clothes were dazzling white. Then the three disciples saw Moses and Elijah talking with Jesus. So Peter spoke up and said to Jesus, "Lord, how good it is that we are here! If you wish, I will make three tents here, one for you, one for Moses, and one for Elijah." While he was talking, a shining cloud came over them, and a voice from the cloud said, "This is my own dear Son, with whom I am pleased—listen to him!"

—Matthew 17:1–5

⠶ STRUCTURE OF PRAYER

Although Dominic only described nine prayer forms in his original work, he implied a tenth and final form known as contemplation. Contemplation is distinct from meditation in that it is the purest, most perfect form of prayer and uses neither words nor mental imagery. In fact, it involves us literally doing nothing and thinking nothing and, instead, allowing God to show us His love. Contemplative prayer is a prayer of silence and listening in which a person is united with God and receives a foretaste of heaven. It is a style of prayer that quietly seeks out God in the silence of one's heart. Meditation (as described in the ninth way) is often, but not always, the stage that leads to pure, beautiful, silent contemplation. This "tenth prayer form" of St. Dominic is also sometimes called the Unitive Way.

It's actually very appropriate that St. Dominic never gave instructions in contemplative prayer or specifically described it in *The Nine Ways of Prayer*. It's very difficult to describe or teach, let alone learn. There are many people who pretend to know a great deal about prayer, but if they equate meditative and contemplative prayer, they don't really understand much. Contemplative prayer is something so completely different from normal living experience that people who pass it off as unimportant or as "easy" betray their ignorance of the subject. Contemplation is as different from the usual forms of prayer as a magnificent, awe-inspiring aria is from simple humming.

Contemplative Prayer: *The Path to Unknowing*

If you desire intimate union with God you must be willing to pay the price for it. The price is small enough. In fact, it is not even a price at all: it only seems to be so with us. We find it difficult to give up our desire for things that can never satisfy us in order to purchase the One Good in Whom is all our joy—and in Whom, moreover, we get back everything else that we have renounced besides! The fact remains that contemplation will not be given to those who willfully remain at a distance from God, who confine their interior life to a few routine exercises of piety and a few external acts of worship and service performed as a matter of duty. Such people are careful to avoid sin. They respect God as a Master. But their heart does not belong to Him.

—Thomas Merton[21]

The easiest way to understand what contemplation is comes from the words of a modern mystic, Blessed Mother Teresa of Calcutta. When she was asked what she says to God in prayer, she responded, "I don't. I listen." And, when the interviewer pressed her and asked what does God say to her in prayer, she responded, "He doesn't. He listens." Contemplation is the highest form of prayer and, understandably, the most difficult to learn and practice. It traces its history to the Desert Fathers of early Christian monasticism. Every other prayer tradition feeds into and supports this one.

The modern, renewed interest in contemplation centers around the writings of Trappist monks who focused on the practice of centering prayer, including Fr. William Meninger, Fr. Thomas Merton, Abbot M. Basil Pennington, and Fr. Thomas Keating. As a result, people sometimes confuse centering prayer with contemplation. In actuality, centering prayer is a stepping-off point for contemplative prayer. Centering prayer is one way of preparing that we can do in order to ultimately stop thinking and let God fill us.

There is a significant difference between the Roman Catholic tradition of centering prayer and the Orthodox Church's concept of hesychasm, but this is not the best forum for such a discussion. Suffice it to say that the principal difference between the two philosophies of prayer is that centering prayer is meant to rid the mind of its own "mindfulness" in order to better experience God in the silence of one's soul. In the Orthodox concept of hesychasm, on the other hand, one's rational faculties are retained so as to best witness and contemplate God's mysteries. The similarities between the two, however, are identical in terms of their practice. Both use controlled breathing, a deadening of the senses, a theological perspective of God as "unknowable," and short repetitive prayer with a heavy reliance upon the Jesus Prayer.

When we truly contemplate, our thoughts and emotions are completely quiet as we commune with God. To get to this level, one needs to dispense with the most precious thing we possess: our ego. When we center ourselves, we prepare ourselves for God so He can teach and transform us. In contemplation, we are silent so that God can speak to us. But, to get to this point, we must first center ourselves, or dispose ourselves, which means we need to consciously remove all mental and emotional distractions, through the other prayer forms discussed in this book.[22]

Contemplation is a prayer of no-prayer. When one contemplates, one uses neither words nor thoughts, neither metaphors nor images. It is not something that is easily accomplished, nor is it for beginners. Our minds are always full of psychic clutter and only a spiritually well-trained mind has shut out that noise to the point of being gifted with true contemplation.

Contemplation is the highest form and the goal of all who pray and seek union with God, or as St. Teresa of Ávila called it, "the art of loving."

It is distinct from meditation, which uses one's senses, emotions, and reason to stimulate the soul, allowing understanding to fill us. Contemplation, strictly speaking, has no goal. It is instead the gift of God—to one who has stripped his mind of its mindfulness. A mind stripped of its reason, memory, and will is finally conducive to direct interaction with Christ. Whereas meditation is self-directed, contemplation is God-directed. Whereas an individual prays orally, the contemplative experiences God praying inside his or her soul.

The contemplative is passive; he has become an emptied vessel in which the Holy Spirit resides. The contemplative gazes, and during contemplation, the sleeper awakens. (See Rom. 13:11.) Pope Benedict XVI referred to St. Joseph,[23] Mary's husband, as a model for those who wish to practice inner silence and prayerful listening in a speech he gave to the 46th World Communications Day on May 20, 2012:

> The silence of St. Joseph is a silence drawn from his contemplation of the mystery of God in an attitude of complete availability to the divine will. In other words, St. Joseph's silence is not a sign of interior emptiness but, to the contrary, of the fullness of the faith he carries in his heart and that guides each of his thoughts and actions. It is a silence due to which Joseph, together with Mary,

keeps the Word of God made known through the Holy Scriptures while confronting them all the time with the events of Jesus' life. It is a silence woven of constant prayer, of prayer blessing the Lord, of adoration of His holy will and of total trust in His providence. Let us allow ourselves to be [infected] by St. Joseph's silence! We have such need of it in a world that is often far too noisy, unsupportive of listening in recollection to the voice of God.[24]

All Prayer Leads Toward Contemplation

A person who prays doesn't change the world. Instead, he changes himself. It's easy to identify those who pray and those who don't. A person who prays will continue to sin, as sin is the natural state of humankind, but it will become harder and harder to do so the more that he prays. Christ invites everyone, Christians and non-Christians, to prayer and to dedicate themselves to Him (Matt. 11:28). As St. Thérèse of Lisieux reminds us:

Jesus wants to possess your heart completely. He wants you to be a great saint. The good God never asks the impossible.[25]

We are a world in desperate need of His love and understanding, not because He refuses to give it to us but because we are resolute in refusing it.

If we were as willing to accept it, it would transform the world around us. We would be mirrors of His love just as He explains in Scripture:

> Jesus spoke to the Pharisees again. "I am the light of the world," he said. "Whoever follows me will have the light of life and will never walk in darkness." (Jn. 8:12)

When we pray, we are reaching out to God, the Author of Love. God's overpowering love is not the same feeble form of love with which humanity is familiar. God's love is the love that holds atoms together, planets in orbit, and galaxies spinning alone in the darkness of space. When prayer leads to contemplation, the soul becomes a mirror for the Holy Spirit, Who is an all-powerful, ego-shattering love.

In contemplation, one's awareness of oneself is replaced by an awareness of the presence of God Himself. Contemplation isn't for everyone, as not everyone is ready for it. But those who are ready know that they are because meditation and other forms of prayer are no longer spiritually satisfying, helpful, or perhaps even enjoyable. Having difficulty remaining attentive during meditation can be a sign of this, but the singularly most important sign that one is ready for contemplation is the realization that simply sitting still and resting in God is the ultimate pleasure.

Abba Joseph of Panephysis, one of the Desert Fathers, offers the earnest Christian in search of developing his or her spirituality the correct understanding of contemplation:

> Abba Lot went to see Abba Joseph and said to him, "Abba, as far as I can I say my little office, I fast a little, I pray and meditate, I live in peace and as far as I can, I purify my thoughts. What else can I do?" Then the old man stood up and stretched his hands toward heaven. His fingers became like ten lamps of fire and he said to him, "If you will, you can become all flame."[26]

One can only approach God with a pure and repentant heart. No one is capable of doing this alone, and so we need to give ourselves over completely to God.

Contemplative prayer will produce in the individual an imperturbable inner peace. He will be granted great personal insight and wisdom. The person becomes extremely humble and more forgiving of others. He comes to understand his compulsiveness, his sins, his failures, and the emotions that cause them. Anger is shed, as is existential fear, and finally the ego. One comes into a state of mindlessness, thus abandoning discursive thought. Once achieved, the soul is free and finally stable. But these spiritual phenomena are only secondary. Resting in God and allowing God to rest in you is the sole "activity" of contemplation. In this transformational relationship we find our true humanity. Our self-love (that is, ego) is our false self.

Contemplation, then, is loving God as our true self. To hope for spiritual gifts such as visions or prophecy is a waste of time and one will quickly become frustrated in that search. These gifts are very uncommon and are never granted if one looks for them; only a humble heart will be thusly rewarded. We should seek the God of Consolations, not the consolations of God. Our dealings with Christ should be as St. Francis de Sales suggests:

> To lose ourselves in God is simply to give up our own will to Him.
> When a soul can truly say, "Lord, I have no other will than Yours,"
> it is truly lost in God and united to Him.[27]

In the contemplative state, we are essentially empty. We allow God to strip us of our narcissism, our active memory, sense data, our emotions, and our logic. We become empty vessels into which the Holy Spirit lavishes His love.

The God who said, "Out of darkness the light shall shine!" is the same God who made his light shine in our hearts, to bring us the knowledge of God's glory shining in the face of Christ. Yet we who have this spiritual treasure are like common clay pots, in order to show that the supreme power belongs to God, not to us. (2 Cor. 4:6–7)

St. John of the Cross also describes this concept beautifully in his *Dark Night of the Soul*.

In this condition, again, souls become submissive and obedient upon the spiritual road, for, when they see their own misery, not only do they hear what is taught them, but they even desire that anyone may set them on the way and tell them what they ought to do. The affective presumption which they sometimes had in their prosperity is taken from them; and finally, there are swept away from them on this road all the other imperfections which we noted above with respect to this first sin, which is spiritual pride.[28]

In true contemplation, we experience absolute trust in the Lord.

So, all prayer forms lead to contemplation, and Christian contemplation is very real, very important. Christian contemplation, however, is not:

Meditation full of imagery. Contemplation is a prayer of silence. When contemplating, one imagines nothing in order to allow God free rein in one's heart.

Omphaloskepsis (Greek for "contemplation of one's navel"). Contemplation is real and it resonates in the rest of one's life. One contemplates in order to live in this world lovingly and faithfully, not to escape the world's problems.

A theory learned from a textbook. Contemplation is a gift from God that one cannot deliberately practice. At the same time, it is a complex and weighty experience and thus one requires a spiritual director for assistance.

A finished and insular theology independent or superseding all other doctrine. Contemplation is not an alternative to learning or believing in the teachings of the Church. In fact, contemplation couldn't exist independent from the faith, nor should anyone think they could simply "skip ahead." It must be no accident that those who receive this tremendous gift seem to always have a thorough understanding of theology, Scripture, and other forms of prayer.

Easy. True Christian contemplation takes a very long time—before we are gifted with it.

Cool or faddish. Contemplation is not something one simply "picks up." It is the natural step after many years of prayer and meditation. It is not something that someone tries and gets bored with. It is life itself.

An excuse for haughtiness, bragging, or other bad behavior. Contemplation transforms people into warm, loving, selfless, and generous individuals. They would actively avoid immodesty and calling attention to themselves.

An esoteric ritual. There is neither magic nor process in contemplation. The only goal is encountering God, which can only be initiated by Him; we are passive before Him.

The equivalent of the experience gained through hypnosis or drugs. If contemplation could be simulated through the use of hypnosis or drugs, every user would be a mystic, saint, and philanthropist.

Something that can be bought. If anyone is charging money to teach contemplation "techniques," I would urge you to run, not walk, away from them. Only God can give the gift of contemplation.

Yoga or spiritual "exercise." You might feel more flexible after a session of yoga, and more spiritually calm after a session of meditation, but you will feel no closer to sanctity than you would if you had run a marathon. In contemplation, the Holy Spirit has filled us. We are found wholly in Him. With this new identity, one can then be a conduit for God's love in the world.

Commonplace. Contemplation is utterly unique. Christian contemplation is unlike anything else in human experience.

✖ HOW TO PRACTICE
How to Dispose Oneself for the Gift of Contemplation

Contemplation is the most perfect form of loving God. The proper end of spiritual enlightenment is God and nothing else. St. Dominic and ancient Christian mystics would see contemplation as a gift given usually after *lectio, meditatio, et oratio*, all disposing for God's gift of Himself. So, then, how do we "achieve" this tenth and final stage of prayer?

We don't, exactly. There is no "How to Practice" in this tenth prayer form. But we may receive this stage as a gift from God. Still, there are ways in which one may dispose oneself to be prepared for this incredible gift.

Contemplation does not come by simply plopping down on the carpet and lolling your time away doing nothing. The principle fruit of contemplation is love. You will know you are successful in your prayer life when you realize you have more compassion for those around you and are less judgmental and more generous. As St. John of the Cross teaches us, "A soul enkindled with love is a gentle, meek, humble, and patient soul." Above all, remember this advice: If you wish to see God, forgive everyone. Anger and resentment are poisons for the spirit, as are all of the deadly sins, but none as bad as pride. The contemplative mind is free of emotions. When contemplation ends, this theocentric orientation becomes permanent in one's life. This is not to say that sin disappears completely. Our sinful natures are still with us, but a contemplative actively avoids sinning just as we actively avoid hurting those we love.

The ultimate purpose of contemplative prayer is to come to the point of "unknowing." With that said, what follows is not at all a how-to guide—but Christian mystics down through the ages will generally agree that these step-by-step instructions represent a synthesis of how one might prepare oneself to reach the contemplative stage of prayer.

1   Find a quiet place, sit comfortably, and close your eyes.

2   Pray the following: "O Lord, open my lips and my mouth will declare your praise" (Ps. 51:15, NRSV).

3   Clear your mind.

4   Pray the following: "My lover speaks to me. Come then, my love; my darling, come with me" (S. of S. 2:10).

5   Breathe deeply and concentrate on your breathing.

6   Step by step, concentrate on relaxing every part of your body.

7   Ignore sense data.

8   Clear your mind of emotions.

9   Get rid of desires and feelings.

10   Use the Jesus Prayer, and other essential, tried-and-true simple prayers, to quiet your mind.

11   Still your imagination.

12   Disregard your active and passive memory.

13   Quiet your mind by not thinking. If stray thoughts come to the forefront, simply push them aside and return to your search for Christ.

14   Allow your narcissism to dissipate.

15   Open yourself to God's love. Feel His presence. Trust in His faithfulness.

16   Actively listen for Christ in your heart. Be open to how He moves you.

17   Do all of this again, and again, and again, for a lifetime. . . .

✖ SCRIPTURE READING

Lord, hear my prayer! In your righteousness listen to my plea; answer me in your faithfulness! Don't put me, your servant, on trial; no one is innocent in your sight. My enemies have hunted me down and completely defeated me. They have put me in a dark prison, and I am like those who died long ago. So I am ready to give up; I am in deep despair. I remember the days gone by; I think about all that you have done, I bring to mind all your deeds. I lift up my hands to you in prayer; like dry ground my soul is thirsty for you. Answer me now, Lord! I have lost all hope. Don't hide yourself from me, or I will be among those who go down to the world of the dead. Remind me each morning of your constant love, for I put my trust in you. My prayers go up to you; show me the way I should go. I go to you for protection, Lord; rescue me from my enemies. You are my God; teach me to do your will. Be good to me, and guide me on a safe path. Rescue me, Lord, as you have promised; in your goodness save me from my troubles! Because of your love for me, kill my enemies and destroy all my oppressors, for I am your servant.

(Ps. 143:1–12)

Thousands of Prayer Forms

No matter how much you dream, how much useless
work you do, or how much you talk, you must still stand
in awe of God.

—Ecclesiastes 5:7

A fter studying these ten prayer forms, some reader might ask, "Is this all there is?" (Then again, most of us have our hands full with these ten!)

There are many other legitimate prayer forms out there, including pilgrimages, nightly recollections, Eucharistic adoration, works of charity, and countless forms and levels of meditation and contemplation. All of these are good. But the ten forms in this book, with God's grace, are a way of growing in sanctity for people of all backgrounds.

Before exploring these other Christian forms of prayer, I suggest that you concentrate on the tried-and-true methods you have encountered in this book, from the fruit of eight hundred years of Dominican wisdom.

*How to
Pray
the
Dominican
Way*

140

Allow them to fill and heal your soul. Empty yourself so that the Holy Spirit may guide you. By so doing, He will remove your heart of stone and give you "an obedient heart" (Ezek. 36:26).

Stick with these prayer forms. Practice them relentlessly for a long time. Flittering nervously and tentatively from one prayer form to another without giving time to explore it thoroughly will only serve to inflame your ego, the exact opposite result of true spirituality. You will know that these prayers are working in your life if you find yourself growing smaller and weaker while He grows ever larger and stronger. (You may need a spiritual director to detect this, in your life, for you.)

Keep in Mind

There are no fast tracks to developing a deep spirituality. The world is full of charlatans of all faiths who present themselves as being "spiritually accomplished"—who will, for a fee, "ply their skills." Those who pay cash for "spiritual enlightenment" should remember the Church Father Tertullian's sage advice: "Nothing that is God's is obtainable by money."

The anonymous author of *The Cloud of Unknowing* repeats this advice and urges the seeker of spiritual truth to go after the experience of love in one's prayer life rather than "mystical knowledge." The prideful seeking of knowledge will deceive you, but the gentle, loving affection whose Source is Christ will never deceive you. Knowledge tends to breed conceit, but love builds and heals. Knowledge is full of labor, but love full of rest.

A real spirituality will liberate you from wants and desires. It replaces them with a desire only to be with God and spend time with Him. No "special skills." No bells and whistles. You must diminish while He increases (Jn. 3:22–30). Do not look for any consolations other than the ultimate joy of being with God—something that isn't attained but rather something God gives us graciously. Again, the author of *The Cloud of Unknowing* teaches:

> The purpose of prayer is the noughting of oneself and the all-ing of God.

Prayer is the only rational response to this inordinate love of self with which we torture ourselves. Humility before God is the medicine that cures stultifying, suffocating pride and reorients the soul toward the only real and important Thing in the universe—faith is a rejection of self-love.

Human beings are unique among all earthly creatures in that we can think rationally and act lovingly—this is what's meant when theologians say we are made in God's image. By releasing our hold upon ourselves and seeking out God in prayer, we come to a better appreciation and understanding of our humanity—both the rational and the loving.

How to
Pray
the
Dominican
Way

142

Prayer is the means by which we seek out the Divinity, and even though it's a slow and tortuous process sometimes, seemingly without making real progress, the truth is, though we initiate it, God is the Mover that carries us forward. We aren't in charge of our progress in spiritual matters, although it can be fairly said we are thoroughly responsible for our regressions and failures—God is the accelerator and we are the brakes. By opening ourselves up and shedding the old self we come to better understand our Creator (Col. 3:9–11). He and He alone guides us through the process of getting to know Him, and it is by His grace and His grace alone that we may succeed in prayer. So, as St. Padre Pio reminds us:

Pray. Hope. Don't Worry.

Then I will go to your altar, O God; you are the source of my happiness. I will play my harp and sing praise to you, O God, my God.

(Ps. 43:4)

Dominican Resources

The Dominican family is made up of three orders, but all Dominicans are united as followers of St. Dominic. All of them pray the Rosary, the Liturgy of the Hours, and attend daily Mass. They also read, study, and contemplate the Bible and other spiritual writings.

First Order Dominicans (http://curia.op.org/en/)

The First Order of Dominicans are priests and brothers. It was the first community founded by St. Dominic in 1216 in order to combat error and ignorance. Their tools were faith, compassion, and knowledge. The motto of the order is *Veritas* (truth) and their sole purpose is to praise God in prayer, adoration, meditation, and contemplation, and to preach His Truth. Thus, the community's second motto, *Laudare, benedicere, praedicare* ("To praise, to bless, to preach").

How to
Pray
the
Dominican
Way

144

Second Order Dominicans
(http://www.usaopnuns.org/)

The second order that St. Dominic created is appropriately named the Second Order of Preachers. Nuns and sisters make up that community. Contrary to popular opinion, there is a difference between a nun and a sister. A religious sister is involved in active ministry in the world. A nun is a cloistered woman who restricts her ministry to within her monastery. They are frequently teachers and scholars, but many are also involved with manual labor necessary to maintain their community.

The Second Order was created in 1206 when Dominic gathered together the Albigensian women converts to the Catholic faith in the monastery of Blessed Mary of Prouille. The Dominican nuns thus were started before the friars. The main task set before cloistered, contemplative Dominican nuns was to pray for the success of the Dominican preachers working against error, ignorance, hatred, and heresy in the world. They pray for the world and for everyone in it.

Dominican sisters are involved in a variety of ministries in many dozens of countries. They, like their male counterparts, combat heresy whereever it is found and witness to the glory, justice, beauty, and compassion of God.

Third Order Dominicans
(http://www.3op.org/)

The Third Order Dominicans are a lay fraternity in the Church that has 80,000 members worldwide. It was started in 1285. Members of the community are referred to as tertiaries. Several saints and blesseds in the Church have been Third Order Dominicans, including St. Louis de Montfort, St. Catherine of Siena, St. Rose of Lima, and Blessed Pier Giorgio Frassati. Though lay men and women in the Fraternities of St. Dominic do not live in community with each other, they are nonetheless dedicated to many of the same spiritual disciplines as Dominican priests, brothers, nuns, and sisters.

Many of the first Dominican tertiaries were ex-Albigensians who reverted to Catholicism. These people, having rediscovered their Catholic faith, wanted a way to always be mindful of their faith, especially when it came to penance. Over the centuries, the tertiaries began to stress the importance for lay Catholics to be knowledgeable about the faith. Originally, the tertiaries also served in a military capacity, physically defending the Church against armed combatants. These days, tertiaries protect the Church through apologetics and catechetics.

In 1285, Munio de Zamora, the seventh Master General of the Dominican Order, at the recommendation of Pope Honorius IV, wrote the

*How to
Pray
the
Dominican
Way*

146

Rule for "The Third Order of Penance of St. Dominic." On January 28, 1286, the pope officially recognized the new fraternity. This Rule covered several basic points, including that the government of the Dominican Fraternities is subject to ecclesiastical authority; the tertiaries should be truly zealous for the Catholic faith; fraternity members should visit and help sick members of the community; and fraternity members should actively keep others in their prayers.

After a postulancy period of six months, a Catholic of either gender can seek admittance to the Dominican Order as a Third Order novice. This is a simple one-year commitment to a formation course, which helps develop the believer's prayer life. During this period, the novice seeks to discern God's will for him or her.

At the end of the one-year commitment, the novice may request to make a temporary three-year profession as a Third Order Dominican. If accepted, the professed Dominican receives the white scapular of the Order and continues to live by the Rule. At the end of the three-year commitment, he or she may renew his or her profession or choose to make a perpetual profession in the Dominican community.

1 Benedict XVI. February 3, 2010. Address at the general audience held in Paul VI Hall.

2 *Libellus de principiis Ordinis Praedicatorum autore Iordano de Saxonia,* ed. H.C. Scheeben. Rome: Monumenta Historica Sancti Patris Nostri Dominici, 1935.

3 Reservation of the Eucharist in a monstrance upon the altar was a later development.

4 Christians don't have "mantras," because mantras technically are meant as "words of power," which embody their power in the actual syllables that compose them. Thus mantras can't be translated from their original languages. The Jesus Prayer, like all other Christian prayers, can be spoken in any language as it holds no other power than its professed meaning and is meant solely as communication with God.

5 The prayer is thoroughly described in the nineteenth-century anonymously written book *The Way of a Pilgrim.* The novel describes a wandering Russian monk who seeks a life of Christian asceticism and specifically seeks to learn how to pray without

How to
Pray
the
Dominican
Way

148

ceasing. It is a stunning spiritual treatise and should be read by every Christian and everyone else who wishes to develop a proper, healthy, and mature spirituality. The prayer also plays prominently in, of all places, J.D. Salinger's novel *Franny and Zooey,* where it takes on the purpose of helping lead Zooey to an enlightened view of the universe and her life.

6 Raffaele Carcano, the general secretary of the Italian Atheist and Rationalist Society, once claimed in a debate with the then-Cardinal Ratzinger, that there were one billion atheists in the world. Putting aside the outrageous overestimation, if one in every seven human beings is an atheist, and the atheist path was able to lead to true virtue, one-seventh of the world's charities would be operated and financially supported by the atheist community. Is that the case? I don't think so. Atheism, in fact, leads away from godliness, self-sacrifice, and true virtue. For atheists to be as generous or as compassionate as Christians, they would have to muster at least as many hospitals, clinics, food pantries, soup kitchens, retirement centers, and schools for poor children, proportionally speaking, as do Christian believers.

7 The second-century Christian apologist Tertullian notes in chapter 33 of his *Apologeticum* that the slave was probably directed to say,

"Respice post te! Hominem te esse memento!" This translates as: "Look behind you! Remember that you are but a man!"

8 Jim Van Vurst, OFM, "Jesus on Fasting and Penance," http://www.americancatholic.org/e-news/friarjack/Newlayout.aspx?id=11. Posted February 11, 2009; accessed May 8, 2012.

9 These two prayers are taken from *Christian Prayer: The Liturgy of the Hours*. New York: Catholic Book Publishing Co., 1976. *Miserere,* p. 907; *De profundis,* p. 147.

10 This quotation is taken from the original *Nine Ways of Prayer*.

11 There actually wasn't a woman named Veronica who wiped Christ's face. The name is derived from the expression *vera iconica,* which means "the true or real icon" and which referred to Christ's image on the unnamed woman's veil.

12 This quotation is taken from the original *Nine Ways of Prayer*.

13 Greek: "self-emptying."

14 Janina Gomes, "Chanting the Rosary: With Faith and Hope," *Times of India,* July 22, 2003.

15 According to Fr. John Vidmar, OP, author of *Praying With the Dominicans,* Dominicans start the Rosary slightly differently, but otherwise their Rosary is identical to the Roman one.

How to
Pray
the
Dominican
Way

150

16 Herbert Thurston and Andrew Shipman, "The Rosary," in *The Catholic Encyclopedia*, vol. 13. New York: Robert Appleton Company, 1912.

17 Kevin Orlin Johnson, *Rosary: Mysteries, Meditations, and the Telling of the Beads*. Dallas: Pangaeus Press, 1997.

18 St. Louis de Montfort, *The Secret of the Rosary*. Charlotte, NC: TAN Books, 1976.

19 I should point out that the Dominican form of the Rosary is actually longer and more complex than the standard one most Christians use. For example, they start the Rosary in the same way they start the Liturgy of the Hours. Further, they don't use the Fatima Prayer at the end of the decade of Hail Marys. Any Dominican priest or sister can teach you this alternative form of the Rosary.

20 Father James Martin, sj, personal correspondence, February 11, 2009.

21 Richard J. Foster, "Thomas Merton," in *Spiritual Classics,* 18–19. New York: HarperOne, 2000.

22 After practicing centering prayer for a while, you will find the ever-increasing need to be interiorly silent to be overwhelming. Instead of the long formula of the Jesus Prayer, you might consider a short word with one or two syllables such as "love," "God," or "Christ."

23 St. Joseph is often referred to as "the Silent One" by scriptural scholars because he was never directly quoted in the Gospels.

24 Pope Benedict XVI. 46th World Communications Day "Silence and Word" Path of Evangelization. Sunday, May 20, 2012.

25 St. Thérèse of Lisieux, *The Story of a Soul,* 3rd Edition, trans. Fr. John Clarke, OCD. Washington, DC: ICS Publications, 1996, p. 221.

26 *The Sayings of the Desert Fathers: The Alphabetical Collection*, trans., Benedicta Ward. Cistercian Studies Series, no. 59, 103. Trappist, KY: Cistercian Publications, 1987.

27 St. Francis de Sales. *Introduction to the Devout Life.* New York: Vintage, 2002, p. 45.

28 St. John of the Cross. *The Dark Night of the Soul*, revised edition, trans., Kieran Kavanaugh, OCD. Washington, DC: ICS Publications, 1991. Chapter 12, section 9.

About Paraclete Press

WHO WE ARE

Paraclete Press is a publisher of books, recordings, and DVDs on Christian spirituality. Our publishing represents a full expression of Christian belief and practice—from Catholic to Evangelical, from Protestant to Orthodox.

We are the publishing arm of the Community of Jesus, an ecumenical monastic community in the Benedictine tradition. As such, we are uniquely positioned in the marketplace without connection to a large corporation and with informal relationships to many branches and denominations of faith.

WHAT WE ARE DOING

Books Paraclete publishes books that show the richness and depth of what it means to be Christian. Although Benedictine spirituality is at the heart of all that we do, we publish books that reflect the Christian experience across many cultures, time periods, and houses of worship. We publish books that nourish the vibrant life of the church and its people—books about spiritual practice, formation, history, ideas, and customs.

We have several different series, including the best-selling Paraclete Essentials and Paraclete Giants series of classic texts in contemporary English; A Voice from the Monastery—men and women monastics writing about living a spiritual life today; award-winning poetry; best-selling gift books for children on the occasions of baptism and first communion; and the Active Prayer Series that brings creativity and liveliness to any life of prayer.

Recordings From Gregorian chant to contemporary American choral works, our music recordings celebrate sacred choral music through the centuries. Paraclete distributes the recordings of the internationally acclaimed choir Gloriæ Dei Cantores, praised for their "rapt and fathomless spiritual intensity" by *American Record Guide,* and the Gloriæ Dei Cantores Schola, which specializes in the study and performance of Gregorian chant. Paraclete is also the exclusive North American distributor of the recordings of the Monastic Choir of St. Peter's Abbey in Solesmes, France, long considered to be a leading authority on Gregorian chant.

Videos Our videos offer spiritual help, healing, and biblical guidance for life issues: grief and loss, marriage, forgiveness, anger management, facing death, and spiritual formation.

Learn more about us at our website:
www.paracletepress.com, or call us toll-free at 1-800-451-5006.

SCAN TO READ MORE

You may also be interested in...

Words of Light Inspiration from the Letters of Padre Pio
St. Padre Pio
Compiled by Fr. Raniero Cantalamessa

If you are interested in the complexities and challenges of contemporary faith, you will benefit from these short teachings, counsels, and recollections culled from some of Padre Pio's most personal writings

ISBN: 9781557256430 | $14.99, Paperback

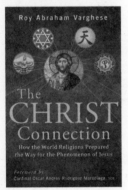

The Christ Connection
Roy Abraham Varghese

"I feel that I can more fully explain the history of my Catholic faith after reading this book."
—RAYMOND FLYNN,
former ambassador to the Vatican, mayor of Boston and political analyst

A noted apologist offers a comprehensive and compelling formulation of the truth that Jesus of Nazareth is both God and man, Messiah and Savior.

ISBN: 9781557256997 | $19.99, Paperback

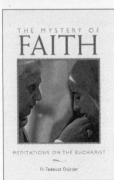

The Mystery of Faith
Fr. Tadeusz Dajczer

This profound book will encourage you to live the Eucharist. First appearing in its original Polish, it quickly sold out of six printings in Poland. Now translated into many languages, *The Mystery of Faith* is impacting Catholic spirituality all over the world.

ISBN: 9781557256867 | $17.99, Hardcover

Available from most booksellers or through Paraclete Press
www.paracletepress.com; 1-800-451-5006. Try your local bookstore first.